The Missionaries of La Salette: From France to North America

By Fr. Donald Paradis, M.S.

Third Edition 2018
Expanded and Updated

Missionaries of La Salette Corporation
915 Maple Avenue
Hartford, CT 06114-2330, USA
website: www.lasalette.org

First edition: June 8, 1992

Second Edition: May 31, 2000

Third (and expanded) edition: December 31, 2018. Note: This expanded edition contains a wider selection of visuals and an expanded and updated chronology. Copyright @ December 12, 2018 by Missionaries of Our Lady of La Salette, Province of Mary, Mother of the Americas, 915 Maple Avenue, Hartford, CT, 06106-2330, USA

Imprimi Potest: Rev. Fr. Rene J. Butler, M.S., Provincial Superior Missionaries of Our Lady of La Salette, Province of Mary, Mother of the Americas, 915 Maple Avenue Hartford, CT 06106-2330, USA

All rights reserved. No part of this book may be reproduced, stored in a retrieval system, or transmitted, in any form or by any means, electronic, mechanical, photocopying, recording or otherwise, without the written permission of La Salette Communications Center Publications, 947 Park Street, Attleboro, MA 02703 USA

Scripture texts in this work, unless otherwise indicated, are taken from the New American Bible with Revised New Testament and Revised Psalms @ 1991, 1986. 1970 Confraternity of Christian Doctrine, Washington, D.C. and are used by permission of the copyright owner. All Rights Reserved. No part of the New American Bible may be reproduced in any form without permission in writing from the copyright owner.

Printed in the United States of America

Editor and author of "For Your Reflection": Fr. Ron Gagné, M.S.

Booklet Design and Digital Formatting: Jack Battersby and Fr. Ron Gagné, M.S.

This and other La Salette titles are available in paper, e-book and audiobook formats at: www.Amazon.com, itunes.Apple.com, and www.lasalette.org

ISBN: 978-1-946956-18-7

Contents

Introduction —i

Chapter One: A Community Come of Age —1

Chapter Two: An Unfinished Revolution —21

Chapter Three: An Inviting New World —41

Chapter Four: A Reconnaissance Mission —50

Chapter Five: A New Beginning —64

Chapter Six: A Time for Everything —83

Chapter Seven: The Past and The Future of Our Present—117

Sources —129

Chronology (1846-2012) —134

Introduction

As its title indicates, this historical sketch chronicles a notable turning point in the history of the Missionaries of Our Lady of La Salette, narrating the transplanting of the Institute from France to the United States a century ago, and recording the antecedents, circumstances and first-fruits of this momentous decision.

The entire story of the La Salette presence in the New World from 1892 through the present would eminently deserve to be told. Constraints of space and time made it plain from the outset, however, that recounting the birth, development and expansion of each of the four American Provinces would represent an overly ambitious, not to say presumptuous, undertaking.

Fr. Donald Paradis, M.S.
(1932-2015)

Limited in scope by design and necessity, the present essay focuses essentially on the period of transition itself. It describes in some detail what the first La Salette settlers left behind in their homeland, what they found waiting for them here, and what hopes and plans they set out to implement in the formative decade following their arrival in the United States.

It traces the La Salette trajectory within the wider sweep of Church and world events at the turn of the century. The account of the Hartford Foundation's progression further unfolds against the backdrop of the beleaguered Congregation's ongoing struggle with France's ruling anticlerical party. It weaves Old World and New World strands together in a Gospel pattern of dying and rising, bringing into dramatic juxtaposition the threat of extinction in France and the thrill of expansion in America.

The history buff in me welcomed the opportunity to loiter at forgotten bookshelves, relished the challenge of sifting through annals, journals, and letters in search of the stuff and substance of a shared history, of a common heritage. The long, meandering road proved not nearly as bewildering and lonely as had been anticipated. Many colleagues had traveled that way before me.

Among them I single out James P. O'Reilly, M.S., and Eugene G. Barrette, M.S., whose labors of love have unearthed data, marshalled facts, established chronologies, rescued men and events from oblivion, translated source materials, and ventured interpretive readings. They find here the grateful acknowledgment of my fraternal indebtedness to them both.

In an earlier draft, these pages found their way into the hands and scrutiny of willing readers. The proofreading assistance, comments, criticisms, and suggestions offered by Raymond G. Cadran, M.S., Roger J. Plante, M.S., and Normand Theroux, M.S., were most encouraging and helpful. Theirs was by no means a thankless task.

The Sermon on the Mount bids us give attention to wings and roots: "Consider the birds of the air ...Think of the lilies of the field ..." (Matthew 6: 26, 28). The deeper and stronger the roots, the higher one may soar!

First Church of Our Lady of Sorrows in Hartford, CT

Chapter One:
A Community Come of Age

Seal of Approval

The definitive approval of their Institute by decree of the Sacred Congregation of Bishops and Regulars on May 14, 1890, put a welcome seal of approval on the valiant efforts the Missionaries of Our Lady of La Salette had expended for nearly four decades. It recognized their proven apostolic zeal, the rapid expansion of their field of endeavor, and the appreciable increase in their ranks, following a dispiriting period of attrition in membership. It confirmed a canonical status consonant with the universal mission the young Congregation had, from the outset, considered to be an essential dimension of the La Salette calling.

There was indeed cause for rejoicing here. The small Community had eagerly ministered to thirty thousand pilgrims annually since May of 1852, when the founding band settled at the site of the Apparition. The humble beginnings, when a primitive mountain shack had served as bedroom, community room, dining room, workroom and parlor, its ill-fitted planks offering a rare view of the starry alpine sky, and its starkness prompting comparison to the stable at Bethlehem, were gratefully called to mind. In fact, those heroic days bore the authenticating stamp of hardship endured for the sake of the Gospel, the sole guarantee of apostolic fruitfulness.

Fr. Bernard Burnoud (1807-1865); from 1852 through 1855 he was the first La Salette Superior

Able administrators and tireless workers both, Bernard Burnoud (1807-1865)—the superior from 1852 through 1855, and Pierre Archier (1815-1899)—the superior from 1856 through 1865, had managed to provide a seemingly endless stream of visitors with mountaintop catering services; oversee the construction of an impressive shrine church, an engineering feat at that altitude and at that time; keep peace among the one hundred and twenty or so Lombard laborers, ensuring their fullest cooperation with Alfred Berruyer (1819-1901), the renowned architect from the prestigious School of Fine Arts in Lyons; all the while tactfully guiding their own colleagues through the various stages of an experiment in apostolic religious life. Daily confessions, processions, Masses and preaching—in itself a feeding of the multitude in the wilderness—completed the picture. It was anything but a still life.

During the winter months the Fathers engaged in the ministry of parish missions. Their services were much in demand. An off-season base of operation in the see city of Grenoble was provided on Rue Saint-Vincent-de-Paul, subsequently renamed Rue Voltaire, a sign among many of shifting times and allegiances. Solemnly dedicated on February 4, 1855, the Chapel attached to their new residence soon attracted an enviable number of worshipers.

Main altar of La Salette Chapel on Rue Joseph-Chanrion in Grenoble in 1870

Standing against a painted backdrop of mountain scenery, the statue of Our Lady wearing her distinctive crucifix provided the visuals: "The Virgin Reconciler, in the midst of this striking panorama, seemed to come up out of the desert toward her people" [Hostachy, 1930: 35]. By turn, her Missionaries lent their Beautiful Lady the fervor of their eloquence, "echoing and interpreting those very words she had come down on earth to speak."

With slight variations, this basic pattern would repeat itself again and again: in 1869, with the inauguration of the Shrine of Notre-Dame de La Salette de Pipet in Vienne; in 1879 with the opening of the Chapel on Rue Joseph-Chanrion in Grenoble; in 1889, when the Congregation took on the pastoral care of the venerable Shrine of Notre-Dame de l'Hermitage in Noiretable. In the mind of these men such chapels and places of pilgrimage were living extensions of the celebrated site where the Mother of God had come in person to voice her urgent appeal. The goal of their preaching was to quicken in their listeners a sense of Mary's caring presence and thus open their hearts to the grace of conversion.

Seeds of the Future

In January 1876, while under diocesan auspices still and without a recruitment program they could call their own, the La Salette Missionaries grappled in earnest with the crucial question of supply and demand. Their ministries were multiplying and thriving. The laborers, however, were few; the same few. Jean Berthier (1840-1908), who had entered the Community as a deacon of the Grenoble Diocese, described the situation in these terms [Berthier, 1884: 6]:

Jean Berthier, M.S. (1840-1908)

> "Crowds flock to La Salette from everywhere by the thousands, sinners are being converted, and there is definite and visible evidence of a spiritual revival. For almost twenty-five years, from 1852 until now, these same Missionaries, recruited among the deacons and priests of this diocese and other dioceses as well, have been preaching missions and retreats and have been blessed in their work by the One who sent them. Their number is far from sufficient, though, to meet

the demands of those pastors who request their services. To make matters worse, vocations to the priesthood are becoming more and more scarce."

He proposed that a school be founded "for boys who, though poor in the things of this world, are rich in the blessing of a vocation to the religious priesthood." He remembered his first visit to the holy mountain and how he himself had heard the call to La Salette "from the lips of the Virgin Reconciler, who befriends children, the workingman, and the common people." Gathered in Grenoble for their first Chapter on January 29 through February 10, 1876, the La Salette Missionaries discussed Berthier's proposal at some length. Sylvain-Marie Giraud (1830-1885), who entertained loftier views about the reorganization of the Institute, opposed it. As a former leader who had keenly felt the lack of personnel, Archier favored it. "For the Institute of his dreams Father Giraud wanted none but the elite among the clergy. The majority desire was more realistic: to open a school for the formation of future missionaries" [Novel, 1968: 30].

On Saturday, January 29, the day the Chapter opened, Giraud resigned the office of superior he had held since 1865 so as to give his colleagues greater freedom in the vexed matter of the community Rule. At the close of the Chapter, Archier was chosen to succeed him and Berthier was among the councilors. The way toward the establishment of the Apostolic School was now clear. One diplomatic step remained to be taken. Would Amand-Joseph Fava (1826-1899), Ordinary of Grenoble since the previous November 18, object to potential encroachments on his own diocesan minor seminary recruitment? On June 13, 1876, the happy occasion of Bishop Fava's first pilgrimage to the holy mountain, Archier rode with him to La Salette. Somewhere between La Mure, where he had met the prelate and been invited to join him in his carriage, and Corps, Archier broached the crucial subject. A missionary bishop in Martinique prior to his appointment to Grenoble, Fava not only granted the permission but added a warm personal endorsement.

The *Annales de Notre-Dame de La Salette* publicized the decision and invited all interested boys to sign up. The response was overwhelming. When classes began on August 5, 1876, there was a waiting list. The energy Berthier had successfully devoted for ten years to the ministry of parish missions, as the Apostolic School's first director, he now invested in twenty children, "nearly as poor as the original pair, drawn to Mary's mountain and called in turn to be heralds of her mercy." After the Christmas holidays the student body moved down to St. Joseph's at Corps, taking up residence in a dilapidated, barn-like structure on a farm that had been purchased in 1860. Hopeful beginnings reminiscent once more of Christ's birth.

Mission to Scandinavia

Expansion at this point took an especially adventurous turn. Gathered at the site of the Apparition on June 18, 1880, the La Salette Community took part in a moving mission departure ceremony. Two brothers, two priests and seven scholastics, "a polar caravan," would soon set out for Scandinavia. Such resonant and unfamiliar place names as Hammerfest, Harstad, Narvik, Tromsd, and Trondheim would join a growing list of La Salette posts and residences.

Converging circumstances accounted for this unexpected development. Msgr. Bernard Bernard (1826-1895), a priest of the Rheims Archdiocese originally, then Prefect Apostolic of Norway and Lapland, had been seeking reinforcements for service in the vast territory entrusted

Bp. Bernard Bernard, M.S. (1826-1895)

to his care. Devoted to the Weeping Mother and aware of the name her missionary sons had made for themselves as apostles, he had one day come knocking at their door. For want of available manpower, however, they had reluctantly turned him down.

His need was enormous. So was his faith in the future of the La Salette Missionaries. Once their prospects had brightened with the opening of the minor seminary in Corps, he renewed his urgent appeal. The timing could not have been better. With Bishop Fava's support, they were then discussing the feasibility and opportuneness of petitioning Rome for international canonical status. Under the impetus of Bernard's entreaties, things moved quickly. Assembled in Extraordinary Chapter on October 8 and 9, 1878, Our Lady's Missionaries agreed to seek papal approval and to take on the Norway Mission. The Chapter Commissioned Sylvain-Marie Giraud and Henri Berthier (1833-1885) to review and modify the text of the Rule for presentation to the Holy See. Archbishops and bishops had provided testimonials, the dossier was assembled, the formal petition was drafted and sent on its way.

For his part Bernard immediately filed a formal request with the *Congregation de Propaganda Fide*. In this instance, Rome acted with unaccustomed dispatch. Propaganda granted its authorization on March 6, 1879, and the terms of a ten-year contract were worked out. On April 18, 1879, the Congregation of Bishops and Regulars issued the laudatory decree conferring *ad experimentum* pontifical right status on the Institute. Bernard personally ratified this alliance between the Prefecture Apostolic of Norway and Our Lady's Missionaries by joining his new coworkers. He received the crucifix on April 25, 1879 and professed his first vows as a La Salette on July 6, 1880.

The Nordic climate, culture and language, far-flung outposts and Lutheran predominance posed a challenge, to be sure. Yet did the men of La Salette show a tremendous adaptive capacity. Their common touch, unassuming ways, warm one-to-one encounters broke through initial diffidence and distrust to achieve a workable, if precocious, ecumenical detente.

The year 1885 stands out in the annals of the Norway venture. In the short span of six months the Missionaries there experienced both the anguish of tragic loss and the elation of rekindled hope. Meeting in Grenoble from January 8 through February 2 of that year, the General Chapter expressed its delight with the growth of the mission and approved the following vote of confidence: [Novel, 1968: 45]: "The Chapter decides that the General Council may, when it deems it opportune, request the erection of provinces in Norway and France. Meanwhile, it grants to Reverend Father Henri Berthier powers analogous to those of a provincial superior."

Returning to his post following the Chapter and a heartening mission appeal tour in his native France, Berthier had boarded the German ship *Norden* in Hamburg. When the British liner *Cumberland* collided with the *Norden* in the North Sea on February 25, he drowned. Alphonse Besson (1852-1944), who was sailing with him to Scandinavia, survived the ordeal. Some six months later, in the first Roman Catholic ordination in Norway since the Reformation, three La Salette Missionaries were ordained to the priesthood in the Sacred Heart Chapel in Trondheim on August 6. Among them was Joseph Vignon (1861-1912).

For reasons of health, Bernard resigned as Prefect Apostolic in 1887. This proved to be a consequential decision. An irreconcilable conflict arose between the pastoral needs of the mission and the requirements of the religious life, so that upon the expiration of the contract the La Salette Missionaries withdrew [Jaouen, 1953: 94]:

> "The new prefect did not share his predecessor's views on religious life. While he welcomed the collaboration of religious, he believed he could deploy them with no regard for the obligations of obedience and community life, assigning them to isolated posts, far from their confreres, without consulting their superiors. This was the source of the problems that led to the recall of the Fathers in 1892."

Oneness in Purpose

Evoked in capsule form here, the history of the La Salette Missionaries in the years 1852 through 1892 is one of steady development and growth, along seemingly random paths. It is the story of changes and change. The character and spirit of a religious institute cannot be fully captured either in its founding moment or in its official documents. The lived experience that embodies them both must be consulted, if we would grasp the intangible reality of the grace they carry. This lived experience and the decisions taken along the way forge character and shape spirit in ways unforeseen, in ways seldom recognized as they are happening, in ways often denied once they have happened.

Early on, a core of La Salette apostolic works emerged: pastoral care of pilgrims, especially but not exclusively, on the holy mountain; preaching parish missions; conducting retreats for clergy, religious and laity; publication of the *Annales*; service in foreign missions; recruitment and formation of candidates. Each of these related explicitly to the Apparition.

By 1851, when the Bishop of Grenoble, Philibert de Bruillard (1765-1860), approved the Apparition, it was widely believed that La Salette was not meant to be just another Our Lady of this or that place, slipping in alongside Notre-Dame du Laus, Notre-Dame de l'Osier, Notre-Dame de Myans—once the initial celebrity and curiosity surrounding it had subsided—to become one more site of local devotion or the focal point of regional pilgrimages. To a man, the pioneer Missionaries were convinced this was true.

Bishop of Grenoble,
Philibert de Bruillard (1765-1860)

The germinal idea that a member of its founding band, François Denaz (1806-1857), conveyed in his letter of August 4, 1855, to Achille Ginoulhiac (1806-1875), de Bruillard's immediate successor as Bishop of Grenoble, postulates an essential and intimate bond between the religious Congregation-to-be and the Apparition. The import and scope of the Apparition were such, he argued, that a purely external link would fail to do them justice. An intrinsic bond, a bond of identification, is rather what he had in mind. A momentous occurrence in the history of the Church and the world, La Salette—as a historical happening—belongs to the past. Given its enduring significance, however, to remember it merely as a bygone event would be inadequate. It must rather be prolonged in time, extended in space and made ever present in its abiding grace and mystery.

How and where is this identification to be brought about" The divine Messenger's purpose in visiting La Salette must, in fact, become the purpose of her Missionaries. Our Lady's aim in coming to La Salette and the aim her Missionaries pledge to pursue in answering her call—in the very act of their coinciding—bring the Congregation to birth and renew its life. In broad terms, such a coinciding in primary purpose effects the union of her Missionaries with Mary: in her zeal for the coming of God's reign and in her motherly concern for straying humanity. In moa concrete terms, it brings about a oneness with Mary in offering a specific remedy for society's ills.

Denaz then ventures to name these ills: "Unless I am mistaken, the ills eating away at society are greed, sensuality, and annoyance with authority in any form. The Missionaries of Our Lady of La Salette must, therefore, counteract these ills by the voluntary detachment, the mortification and penance, and the absolute obedience of their own lives" [Jaouen, 1953: 36]. In his view, this remedy cannot be something apart from themselves, something they would go about prescribing. Denaz saw the witness of their vowed selves as a prophetic challenge and healing gift to the world. The premise here rounds out his concept of oneness in purpose with Mary. While her Apparition did propose concrete remedies, the Mother of Jesus, first and foremost, brought herself to La Salette, the fullest exemplification of the evangelical counsels.

Resurgence of Prophecy

Pope Pius IX (1792-1878)

The fruit of personal reflection, François Denaz's insightful linkage of La Salette with contemporary evils was the child of mid-nineteenth-century religious thought as well. The unparalleled political upheaval and social turmoil that characterized the period were frequently described in the imagery of sickness, wounds, and violent storms. In times of calamity the Christian people had unfailingly turned to the Mother of their Lord, enlisting the protection of her intercession. In this excerpt from his Encyclical *Ubi Primum* of February 2, 1849, on the Immaculate Conception, an embattled Pope Pius IX (1792-1878) rehearses the trials of the times yet sounds a hopeful note [Doheny, 1954: 3]:

> "In our own day, with the ever-merciful affection so characteristic of her maternal heart, Mary wishes through her efficacious intercession with God, to deliver her children from the sad and grief-laden troubles, from the tribulations, the anxiety, the difficulties and the punishments of God's anger, which afflict the world because of people's sins. Wishing to restrain and dispel the hurricane of evils which, as We lament from the bottom of Our heart, are everywhere afflicting the Church, Mary desires to transform our sadness into joy."

The faithful had formerly turned toward her in their need; it seemed that Mary was now turning toward them in a particularly grave hour, adding to that of her unceasing intercession a Marian ministry of intervention. In his Pastoral Letter of May 1, 1852, announcing the building of a shrine church at La Salette and the establishment of a diocesan missionary corps, de Bruillard draws on this interpretation of recent apparitions and highlights the timeliness of our Lady's visit to the diocese [Bassette, 1955: 276]:

> "Was not this Apparition of September 19, 1846, the presage of the most momentous events? Observe the popular agitation, the toppled thrones, Europe in upheaval, society sliding toward its ruin. Who has preserved us and who will go on preserving us from even greater misfortunes, if not She who came from on high to our mountains to plant there a sign of hope and salvation, a luminous beacon, a bronze serpent toward which devout souls have raised their eyes to forestall heaven's wrath and to heal us of incurable wounds?"

The series of nineteenth-century apparitions on French soil—Paris (1830), La Salette (1846), Lourdes (1858), Pontmain (1871) and Pellevoisin (1876)—was a dramatic resurgence of the charism of prophecy in the Church and hailed as the dawn of the Age of Mary. In his *Commentary on Matthew XI. 13*, St. Thomas Aquinas had written: "The prophet is sent for a twofold purpose: to establish the faith and to redress morals. Now, the faith has been established since through Christ all the promises were fulfilled. For the purpose of correcting morals, however, prophecy is neither wanting nor shall it ever be wanting." Days darkened by godlessness and political turbulence doubtless warranted a fresh outpouring of prophetic light mediated in this decisive instance by the Queen of Prophets herself.

Making Sense of Chaos

Current events were indeed generating confusion. Books and pamphlets of apocalyptic inspiration proliferated in this chaotic period. Countless attempts were made to bring past, present and future together in a comprehensible, albeit contrived, relationship. The Enlightenment, the French Revolution, the Bourbon Restoration, the Paris Commune took on eschatological significance. Many strained to view such trying moments in history as part of a providential plan for the salvation of France and of the world. Ancient prophecies, foretelling an era of prosperity for church and state, ushered in by

the return of a French king and an angelic pope, joining forces to create a universal Christian empire, revived and found an avid readership.

Prominent among such popular apocalypses was the Secret of Melanie Calvat (1831-1904). Divulged piecemeal and in limited circulation as early as 1860, it was published in its entirety in 1879 with the imprimatur of the Bishop of Lecce, Salvatore Zola (1822-1898), her spiritual director. La Salette inevitably became embroiled in the furor its publication unleashed. The dissemination of Melanie's purported secret drew unhealthy attention to the confidences that had been entrusted to (lie two children in the course of the Apparition, but that had hitherto been considered personal in nature and destined always to remain secret. The public message and the secret message of La Salette now stood in sharp distinction.

"What They Don't Tell You at La Salette!" the title of one polemical brochure taunted. While they were careful to say nothing that might impeach her testimony as a witness to the Apparition, the Missionaries dissociated themselves from Melanie's misguided foray into prophecy. Her partisans castigated them for their timid performance as prophets. They were variously denounced for hiding under a bushel basket—supposedly in craven deference to Rome's fear of the *truth*—the more incisive and salutary portion of what Our Lady had revealed.

Her Missionaries stood in a cross fire, fending off the fervid defenders of The Shepherdess, all the while reassuring those who now doubted her credibility as a witness. The drawn out dispute had, in fact, caused a number of people to question the authenticity of the Apparition itself.

A charismatic gift, the message of La Salette belonged to the Church. Our Lady's Missionaries never claimed to be either its proprietors or sole interpreters, but they had every intention of remaining its faithful trustees. They would hand it on in its original integrity. If anything, the controversy confirmed them in their stewardship and challenged them to c it. Biblical in inspiration, prophetic in tone, its urgency lay not in a future stripped of mystery by arcane speculation, but in a present graced by an urgent call to conversion and the most tender assurance of forgiveness.

Learning from Lived Experience

Sharply divergent views concerning the style of religious life—active-apostolic or contemplative-penitential—they should adopt had, from the very beginning, polarized the Community and stymied every attempt to formulate a Rule all the members might truly call their own. On his appointment as superior in May of 1865, Archier immediately referred this embarrassing impasse to the Grenoble chancery. In a written reply, dated June 17, 1856, Philippe Orcel (1805-1878), Vicar General and Rector of the Major Seminary, who had assisted several congregations of religious women in drafting their constitutions, offered this wise advice [Hostachy, 1930: 44]:

> "Have a look at what the experiment has taught you, and then, once you have discussed this with your confreres, especially with the Council, present the outcome of your reflection and of your experience to His Excellency."

(from left) Frs. Rousselot and Orcel

The fruitfulness of the process first becomes apparent in the Rule of 1858, the primitive Rule. Chapter 1 addresses the question of identity in these words [Stern, 1968: 8]: "The Missionaries of Our Lady of La Salette are to consider themselves the messengers of the Queen of heaven ...disseminating and making known, more so by their example than by their words, the divine warnings she herself graciously brought to earth." This self-understanding embraces Mary's purpose in visiting La Salette. The reference to "divine warnings" highlights the Apparition's prophetic dimension. The insert "more so by their example than by their words" emphasizes the spirit of prayer and penance that should spark the Missionaries' zeal and give witness to their continual conversion of life.

Chapter 4 describes the spirit of the Congregation in three-dimensional terms: "men of prayer, men of zeal, men of penance." Under the middle heading we find the first mention in official La Salette documents of "contemporary evils" [Stem, 1968: 10]:

> "Men of zeal, ... they will doubtless give forceful and solid instructions on all the truths of Christianity, but they will especially stress the practical points included in her divine warnings, which are singularly suited in character to the present evils of Christian society, and which, in keeping with Heaven's own designs, cannot fail to be particularly efficacious in touching and converting."

Consultation with their own personal experience taught the La Salette Missionary band of the late 1850s several valuable lessons. Evils were rampant. Society was infected. Such evils could not simply be denied, bemoaned, or ignored. The merciful Apparition challenged its heralds to counteract them. The preaching they had done, the confessions they had heard gave compelling testimony to the fact that hearts could be moved, that lives could be changed. They consequently made it their aim "to rouse sinners from their unfortunate somnolence." They chose preaching by example and by word as their privileged vehicle. They drew their sermon themes from Mary's tearful supplication. They underscored the "practical points" of her Discourse, highlighting their "appropriateness to the times" and welcoming their proven power to "touch and convert." In an age of doomsayers, they resolved to plumb the depths of penance and prayer in search of words their world really needed to hear, words of hope.

Prescribing for Society's Ills

Sylvain-Marie Giraud (1830-1885) at 35 years of age

Sylvain-Marie Giraud, who professed a deep love for the Mother of Christ, faulted the Marian piety of his day for its superficiality [Giraud, 1946: 55]: "What do we too often see? An entirely external devotion that is hardly beneficial, a vague devotion that is unfortunately fostered by a plethora of publications—lacking a solid basis, bereft of theology—from which pure and sound Christian truths are almost always excluded to make room for a naive sentimentality that provides no serious food for thought and leaves the heart empty of firm resolve for doing good."

The widespread rebirth of devotion to the Mother of God, he attributed in large measure to the nineteenth-century apparitions. Precisely because a crisis in history had prompted these visions, he argued, the emerging devotion must intensify the faith commitment of the devotees and spur them to action that will influence the times. Having placed a fair amount of blame for this pitiable state of affairs at the feet of authors, in the autumn of 1861 Giraud undertook his first writing project, *The Book of the Spiritual Exercises of Our Lady of La Salette*.

As the title clearly indicates, the work was patterned after the *Spiritual Exercises* of St. Ignatius Loyola. Drawn from the Discourse and symbolism of La Salette, the points for meditation provided "serious food for thought." The Ignatian dynamic of total engagement of mind, memory, sense, and affect, called for in the contemplations and colloquies, would not "leave the heart empty of firm resolve for doing good," as other approaches obviously had.

On the premise that the Apparition at La Salette signals critical times, Giraud insisted that fleeting moments of fervor fall short of an appropriate response to its urgency [Giraud, 1946: 397]:

> "La Salette is not what the outer eye perceives and marvels at perhaps. It is not simply a shrine where one might spend a few days in recollection and peace. Neither is La Salette that ready emotion that the memory of the tears the Queen of Heaven shed here for sinners quickens in the soul. La Salette is not a few extra prayers offered before the altar, nor a few pious thoughts and holy desires such as visit the soul to mislead us and beguile our pride without really making us better persons."

His survey of the contemporary scene, not surprisingly, includes an unsparing look within the Christian Community itself [Giraud, 1946:51]:

> "What can listless, fickle, lukewarm souls offer this superficial and faithless century? Little else than a depleted Christianity, religious practices without impact, and a devotion devoid of vigor, depth or vitality."

Whereas Denaz had listed three principal ills, reminiscent of the classic trilogy presented in 1 John 2:16, Giraud takes his cue from Our Lady's opening statement and targets unrestrained freedom as the root evil [Giraud, 1946: 397]:

> "La Salette is God, jealous, where the love of souls is concerned, attempting once more—and perhaps for the last time—to win the world back to himself in order to save it;

and who for this reason sends his own Mother, the Mother of a thankless people to weep there and, in her overwhelming sorrow, to thrust upon the world the very threat that pierced her own heart: *If my people refuse to submit, I shall be forced to let fall the arm of my Son.* It is obvious to those whose eyes are open that a dreadful evil has overtaken our modern society, a rebellious spirit, a disregard for authority, and a vehement yearning for absolute independence and unrestrained freedom. La Salette is the divine plan of the Incarnation, distorted and thwarted in its deeply desired fulfillment by people's malice, put before human freedom anew."

References to divine anger and punishment are not absent from his lexicon, yet Giraud founds his appeal on love rather than on the fear of impending chastisement:

"... so much love should entice this liberty of ours to submit freely, humbly, lovingly and respond to so great a love with all the love within our power."

Love and liberty are inextricably bound up. The spirit of the world, however, threatens to maim and paralyze frail human freedom in ways that too often go undetected:

"La Salette is a courageous and energetic protest, a tireless struggle against the deplorable but clever incursions of the world's spirit, before which almost all of us, priests and faithful alike, have been weak until now."

In proposing that the testimony of their own consecrated lives offers the most effective antidote by far to society's chief ills, Denaz focused on who, specifically, the La Salette Missionaries are. Suggesting that they are commissioned to minister to human freedom, diverted from its true goal in every age by cultural incursions, Giraud addresses the related question of what, precisely, the La Salette Missionaries do. Inasmuch as Christ's disciples are to live their lives in loving response to the world's deepest needs, needs manifested in its gravest ills, the world, ironically, does set the Christian agenda.

For Your Reflection

Note: Fr. Ron Gagne, M.S., the editor of this publication, has added the following scripture passages, reflection questions and prayers to each chapter of this book. These are for your personal reflection or as faith sharing opportunities for those who have read this book.

Scripture: Matthew 6: 25-30 (Dependence on God)

> "Therefore I tell you, do not worry about your life, what you will eat [or drink], or about your body, what you will wear. Is not life more than food and the body more than clothing? Look at the birds in the sky; they do not sow or reap, they gather nothing into barns, yet your heavenly Father feeds them. Are not you more important than they? Can any of you by worrying add a single moment to your life-span? Why are you anxious about clothes? Learn from the way the wild flowers grow. They do not work or spin. But I tell you that not even Solomon in all his splendor was clothed like one of them. If God so clothes the grass of the field, which grows today and is thrown into the oven tomorrow, will he not much more provide for you, O you of little faith?"

Questions for reflection:

We have just read about the earliest years of the foundation and growth of the Missionaries of Our Lady of La Salette.

- What major challenge or transition have you, your family, or your parish community been called to deal with in the distant or more recent past?

- When have you seen God's grace at work in yourself or others with regard to challenges in relationships, health or age?

Prayer:

Mary, Mother of Compassion, your assuring words at La Salette concerning blessings from God "if (we) are converted" encourages us to deal courageously with the many challenges we are asked to face in our lives. Your Son urges us not to be anxious when needs arise. We must learn from the way the wild flowers grow.

Help us, loving Mother, to respond to challenges with faith that God will provide for us as difficulties arise. Give us the deep and lasting hope that St. Paul speaks of when he says: "Rejoice in hope, endure in affliction, persevere in prayer."

We ask this through your loving intercession and through the grace of your Son who lives with the Father, and the Holy Spirit, one God, for ever and ever. Amen.

La Salette Invocation:

Our Lady of La Salette, Reconciler of Sinners, pray without ceasing fir us who have recourse to you.

This shows the La Salette Basilica
before the construction of the two towers;

Chapter Two:
An Unfinished Revolution

Progress Unrestricted

As a journalist with *Le Temps*, Jules Ferry (1832-1893) was noted for the lucid analysis and penetration he brought to his commentaries on contemporary events. A century of political strife had scarred the nation with division and polarization. The challenge confronting France, as he saw it, was not unlike the one the United States was facing in its attempt to build a national identity following the Civil War. He believed the unfinished Revolution of 1789 held the key to France's elusive unity. He subjected religion to a ruthless diagnosis and found it "decadent beyond all remedy." The old beliefs had been undermined, he contended, but were being artificially shored up by superstitions more recently concocted, such as Marian apparitions. Ferry concluded that the Church's century-long resistance to the Revolution must be brought to a halt.

Jules Ferry (1832-1893)

Elected to the National Assembly in 1869, Ferry gained a prominent pulpit from which to propound the new humanism. To the cheers of his fellow deputies on the Left, he delivered a fiery speech on April 10, 1870, which set forth the doctrine of unlimited human perfectibility and hailed the ultimate demise of religion [Zeldin, 1973: 625]:

"We shall be truly emancipated when Humanity no longer appears to us as a fallen race, stricken with original sin, but as a ceaseless cavalcade marching forward toward the light. Then shall we experience ourselves as part of the great Being, which cannot perish, Humanity, continually redeemed, developing, improving."

When asked to sum up his ambitions as a legislator and public servant, he replied decisively: "My aim is to reorganize humanity without God and without King."

Engineered Secularization

On September 4, 1870, as France surrendered to Prussia National Assembly Deputy Leon Gambetta (1838-1882), at the head of a mob of revolutionaries, proclaimed the Third French Republic. It proved to be one of the most confusing and paradoxical of all political regimes in any land [Shirer, 1969: 35]:

> "It is a wonder it was born at all. ... It came into being by a fluke. The National Assembly, elected in 1871 after the debacle of France's swift and humiliating defeat by Prussia, had not wanted a republic. Nearly two thirds of its members—some 400 out of 650 deputies were Monarchists. But they could not agree on a king. Some wanted the Comte de Chambord, the legitimate Bourbon heir; others wanted the Comte de Paris, the Orleanist pretender. A few hoped for the return of still another Bonaparte."

Most of the bishops and priests were Monarchists. A natural enough political affiliation, since the pretenders to the throne had affirmed their loyalty to the Church while the Republican leaders were avowed anti-clericals. Government policy regarding the temporal domain of the Pope, by and large, determined the position taken by clergy and laity on Church-State relations. Catholic opinion strongly favored the reestablishment of the Papal States even at the cost of going to war against Italy.

The 1876 election netted the Republicans the parliamentary majority they had long awaited. To secure this Leftist victory, they launched a defensive against the pervasive influence the Church still wielded through its charitable works, preaching and schools. Credit for outstanding effectiveness in each of these areas was given—accurately enough, but reluctantly—to France's men and women religious.

The Republican leadership adopted a graduated secularization plan: establish a mandatory lay primary education system, oust the religious from public and private schools, suppress the Catholic universities, legalize divorce, delimit the respective roles of church vestry and municipality, mandate compulsory military service for seminarians, restore the Pantheon to secular use, abolish public prayers for the National Assembly, bring about the separation of Church and State in due course.

While Gambetta concentrated on foreign policy, Ferry preferred to further his national unity goal as Minister of Education. He worked tirelessly for an entire decade to enact a massive reform that would affect education at every level. Paul Bert (1833-1886), professor of physiology at the Sorbonne, elected to the Chamber of Deputies in 1872, lent his own brand of messianic fervor to the cause of obligatory military service for all.

Phantom Population

During 1878, a census was taken of a legally nonexistent population. This official head count of phantom people yielded astonishing results. There were 30,000 men and 128,00 women religious in France. Regular clergy outnumbered their secular counterparts three to one. Despite the Restoration period decree prohibiting them from teaching, the Jesuits had 60 houses and numbered 1,800. The combined real estate and financial holdings of the religious in France were estimated at 628,000,000 F, a highly inflated figure.

When Ferry introduced his education reform bill on March 15, 1879, he managed to catch even his colleagues unawares by attaching to it a rider that became famous as Article Seven: "None shall be permitted to direct a school of any kind, whether public or private, or engage in any teaching whatsoever who are members of an unauthorized religious community." The rationale was succinctly stated: "Ours is a free and lay state. Education sponsored by clergy and religious derives its inspiration from principles that directly oppose its existence and constitute a peril to its future."

The juridical standing of religious institutes in France was confusing, to say the least. The Revolution had banned religious life outright and forbidden the profession of vows. With time, however, most of the disbanded orders had regrouped and new ones were founded. A source of consternation in the anticlerical camp, this steady growth did not entirely suit all the bishops either. International congregations were thought to enjoy special favor with the Roman Curia. Order priests—Dominicans and Jesuits in particular—were sought after as orators and confessors and, therefore, perceived as competing with the diocesan clergy for influence and benefactions among the faithful.

Napoleon Bonaparte in 1792 by Henri Félix Emmanuel Philippoteaux (1815–1884)

Napoleon I (1769-1821) had purposely omitted any reference to the religious in the 1801 Concordat he concluded with the Holy See. His imperial decree of 1804 had introduced a distinction between authorized and unauthorized congregations: " ... both exist at the sufferance of the state, their members and properties are subject to a foreign power, and they can hardly be described as friendly toward the institutions of their own country. An unauthorized congregation that so requests may be juridically authorized by legislative act, thereby becoming a civil person, subject to state inspection and audit, and acquiring the legal rights and privileges consonant with said status. An unauthorized congregation is bereft of juridical standing and can claim no rights and prerogatives whatsoever. An outlaw, it continues to exist, own property and engage in legal transactions at its own peril" [Gallon, 1972: 239].

The government seldom granted the request; and for all practical purposes, Napoleon's "Organic Articles" had become dead-letter laws. Over the years, therefore, few congregations had troubled to request authorization.

Anticlerical Flares

Article Seven sparked heated debate in the Chamber. The Left was quick to single out the Society of Jesus. The conduct and theology of its members came under attack. They were accused of constituting a state within the state and dubbed "the counterrevolutionary militia." The Right observed that very few of the orders in France had a generalate outside the country, praised the religious for their patriotism, and called attention to their distinguished service as chaplains and unpaid hospital orderlies during the Franco-Prussian War. A petition, bearing a million and a half signatures and urging the repudiation of Article Seven, put the lawmakers on notice that, while anti-clericals had become an established feature of French life, not all anti-clericals were militant. The measure carried, nevertheless, and was sent to the Senate.

Charles de Saulces de Freycinet (1828-1923): photo : Nadar (1820-1910)

Arguing that Republican party rashness had destroyed two Republics in the past, the Senate threatened to reject Article Seven. Speaking for Ferry, Charles de Freycinet (1828-1923), the Prime Minister, warned that if the Upper Chamber voted down the controverted rider his government would be compelled to "apply the existing law." On March 9, 1880, the Senate nonetheless rejected Article Seven. The Chamber retaliated on March 29, voting 324 to 125 to dissolve all the unauthorized congregations. The Jesuits were to vacate their houses within three months. All other unauthorized congregations were to request authorization within ninety days or suffer the same fate eventually.

That very day the Paris police raided eleven religious houses. The Carmelite Friars told them their founder had obtained authorization from Jehu. "Jehu? I can't seem to place him," the mystified gendarme replied. "But I'm not really surprised. These ministers have been playing musical chairs of late."

Coming together on April 27 at the Paris Oratory, the superiors of 48 unauthorized congregations opted to make common cause with the Society of Jesus and voted unanimously not to seek authorization. Whether the Missionaries of Our Lady of La Salette sent a representative to this meeting is unkown.

On June 29, 1880, when the grace period expired, the Jesuits were forcibly expelled from their houses in Paris and in the provinces before sympathizing crowds of bystanders. Four hundred magistrates—many of whom were Jesuit alumni— resigned rather than enforce the decree. Edmond Rousse (1817-1906), a renowned Parisian jurist, drafted an opinion that upheld the unauthorized congregations' right to exist—as rooted in the principles of individual liberty and inviolability of domicile—and their right to live in common—as founded on the provision of Article 291 of the Penal Code, which forbade associations of more than twenty persons unless they were living in the same house. Hundreds of lawyers signed it.

By way of rebuttal, René Waldeck-Rousseau (1846-1904), an attorney and Deputy from Rennes, offered an unabashed articulation of Republican jurisprudence [Galton, 1972: 238]:

> "The State has a bounden duty to guarantee individual rights.

But these rights are abdicated by persons who enter religious orders, into which they are not admitted except by the vows of poverty, obedience and chastity. When you subtract from the human personality that which enables it to possess, that which makes it a reasonable being, and that which enables it to propagate, I ask you how much of that personality remains. Desires and intentions are not strengthened in congregations by cooperation as they are in ordinary associations, but they are annihilated for the benefit of a power whose interests may be contrary to those of the State."

Hoping to ease the tense situation, Charles Lavigerie (1825-1892), Archbishop of Algiers, approached the French Prime Minister that September in the name of Leo XIII (1810-1903). If the religious were willing to state that their refusal to petition authorization was not politically motivated, de Freycinet conceded, execution of the government decree might at least be deferred. Lavigerie then drew up, in behalf of the unauthorized congregations, a declaration that repudiated "all solidarity with political passions" and expressed "submission to the government." Acting on the advice of Hippolyte Guibert (1803-1886), OMI, Archbishop of Paris, they all declined to sign it. Lavigerie, who had been delegated by the Pope to initiate a *rapprochement (reconciliation)* between the Church and the Third Republic, reported his disappointment to the Vatican.

Bp. Charles Martial Allemand Lavigerie (1825-1892), member of the White Fathers

Leo XIII indicated that he would be pleased should the religious endorse such a declaration, but that they remained entirely free to do so or not. Most of them yielded, though quite unwillingly. Resentful of this flirtation with the abhorred Republican regime, a Royalist bishop leaked word of the secret negotiations to the Bordeaux Monarchist newspaper La Guyenne and the deal fell through. The anti-clericals were furious and forced de Freycinet's resignation. Ferry succeeded him as Premier. Without delay, the congregations were notified that the decrees of expulsion would be implemented on schedule. To the grief and outrage of Catholics, 5,643 religious were expelled, and 261 residences were closed in October and November of 1880.

Pope Leo XIII
(in his later years)

The London Times editorialized: "The sympathies of France and of the world will always be on the side of the oppressed. The treatment recently inflicted upon the unauthorized orders in France is generally condemned by impartial judges as an act of despotism." To which Bert retorted: "Let *The Times* concern itself with the Irish and not with us."

False Alarms

Twelve young men received the habit of Our Lady's Missionaries at La Salette on June 21, 1880, three days after the impressive Norway mission departure ceremony. When they came down the mountain to St. Joseph's in Corps, they put aside cassock, cincture and crucifix "to foil the police." Throughout the summer Jean Berthier remained on the alert for any sign that his beloved Apostolic School might be forced to shut its doors. A local Community journal entry records student reaction to the menacing government edict: "If they mean to drive us away, far better they should put us to death than cast us out into the world."

Though the situation was hardly life-threatening, there were a few false alarms and one close call that tense autumn when members of unauthorized congregations, including the La Salette Missionaries, faced the unwelcome prospect of banishment from classroom and homeland. An order aimed at closing the school in Corps was, in fact, issued. The local police chief, who was fond of La Salette, informed Berthier on the sly. Preparations for a hasty evacuation were made. The order was subsequently cancelled, however. The Apostolic School on Rue Chanrion in Grenoble, founded in August of 1879, likewise went unmolested.

The Bishop of Grenoble, it was later learned, had "intervened higher up." Exploiting the word *Missionaries* in the Congregation's title, Fava had convinced the authorities that most of the candidates in training would go on to serve in foreign fields. The Republicans were, in fact, somewhat partial to those men's Institutes that fell under three classifications: "harmless" like the Trappists who remained as silent about politics as they did about everything else; "socially useful" like the Brothers of St. John of God, who cared for the physically and mentally ill; "politically useful" like the Paris Foreign Mission Society and the Missionaries of Africa, who labored in French colonial Indochina and North Africa respectively.

Evidence that anticlericalism was a political tool in the hands of the Left is found in Gambetta's praise of the White Fathers, whose work he considered to be "'worth an army corps to France in Algeria.' When someone commented that this 'sang a different tune from the old battle cry,' Gambetta replied, 'That was a matter of domestic politics; anticlericalism, you know, is not one of our exports'" [Acomb, 1967: 72].

Signs of Appeasement

The 1880s saw some signs of appeasement in Church-State relations. In 1883, Charles Maret (1805-1884), titular Bishop of Sura and respected Dean of the Sorbonne's Theology Department published *La Verité catholique et la paix religieuse (Catholic Truth and Religious Peace)*, in which he suggested that the Church's major challenge was not the Third Republic but the reconciliation of freedom with religion:

> "The clergy should be convinced that the remedy for the

evil which is at work in our society in political forms is not politics. Everything which favors the reign of light, justice, charity, peace, everything which contributes to the reconciliation of science with faith, of freedom with religion, should be the object of the clergy's aspirations."

Departing from his largely ceremonial role and in response to papal overtures, the President of the Republic, Jules Grevy (1807-1891), appealed in writing that same year to Leo XIII [Acomb, 1967:42]:

"Your Holiness rightly complains of anticlerical passions. They certainly exist, together with the opposing sentiments of the majority of the French people. But can one fail to recognize that these passions, which I condemn, have been the product chiefly of the hostile attitude of a part of the clergy toward the Republic, either upon its establishment or in the struggles it has since had to carry on for its existence?"

In an impassioned speech he gave in the Chamber of Deputies on November 6,1886, Raoul Duval (1832-1887) exhorted his fellow Catholics on the Right to abandon their futile obstructionism and begged them to "accept a form of government which you perhaps have not chosen but which leaves you complete freedom to pursue your cause by means of honest and persevering discussion. The Republic belongs to all, to me, to you. It is yours if you will only take your place in it."

Satirical Portrait of Edgar Raoul-Duval (1832-1887) by Léon-Charles Bienvenu

A number of French bishops began to address the issue of Church and State openly. Guilbert of Gap stated: "The early Christians accepted Nero. It is our duty to ensure that the altar does not go down with the throne." Pie of Poitiers countered: "Christ alone is King. It is the duty of the State to listen to the Church as the devout laity listen to their confessor."

Adolphe Perraud (1828-1906), bishop of Autun dared touch upon the social reform both Church and State seemed to be neglecting: "Priests should keep out of political intrigues because the social question calls for their full attention. Lazarus is at our gate (Luke 16:20)." Freppel of Angers, a member of the Chamber of Deputies, insisted: "In a Christian people, politics is but the application of morality to the government of the country, and morality is inseparable from religion" [McManners, 1972: 56].

Adolphe Perraud (1828-1906), bishop of Autun, France; Wikimedia: HDL85

Lavigerie of Algiers called for a redefinition of the Church's primary function in the world: "The role of the Church is the conversion of individuals rather than the Christianizing of society by manipulating governments." Agent of Leo XIIIs conciliatory policy though he was, Lavigerie was excoriated in many quarters. And the Pope's own statement that "Catholicism is not wedded to any one form of government" prompted at least one convent of cloistered nuns "to pray for the conversion of the Holy Father."

Legislative Shuttlecock

Neither was the Republican choir singing in perfect harmony. The Party—an agglomeration of groups and individuals, really—had splintered into Left, Radical Left, Extreme Left and Socialist Left. Majorities were harder to come by; forming and holding parliamentary coalitions, more challenging. "Idealism versus politics" fired many an internal debate. The politicians reminded the ideologues that reform must always be distinguishable from revolution, and cautioned them not to ruffle the upper classes, who wanted only peace and prosperity, or disappoint the lower classes, who wanted only steady jobs and retirement security. Moreover, intense personal rivalries grew apace with the divergence of political views.

In disagreement on fundamental issues such as economic reform and labor legislation, the Republicans were constrained to seek what united them. They found it in anticlericalism, though there was little genuine unanimity about what constituted a realistic anticlerical policy or how relentlessly it ought to be pursued.

And so, anticlerical vexation was designed primarily as a substitute for significant social legislation. It was "the only revolutionary drum the Republicans could beat to evoke memories of 1789 and attract votes without having to put their hands in their pockets to pay for social reforms. In the end that was why clericalism had to be the enemy" [McManners, 1966: 32].

Jean Jaurès in 1904 by Nadar (1820-1910)

In a secular version of Perraud's "Lazarus at the Gate" summons, Jean Jaurès (1859-1914), the formidable Socialist leader, warned against holding popular hopes for liberty, equality and fraternity hostage to parliamentary stalling: "You have torn the people away from the guidance of the Church. You have interrupted the age-old cradle song that lulled human misery. Human misery has reawakened. It is crying, demanding its place in the sunshine of the world."

As a prime instance of anticlerical harassment, the National Asembly bandied back and forth for nearly a decade and a half the exemption from military service of young male religious and seminarians. The Army Law of 1872 had made five years of military service compulsory. Enacted in the days of Monarchist majority, it had exempted the following: public school teachers; members of teaching orders, willing to serve in public or private education for ten years; and seminarians who had taken major orders. On August

4, 1876, Bert introduced legislation reducing the tour of duty to one year and striking all exemptions. His colleagues on the Left required that all should serve the full five years. To ward off such radical excesses the Prime Minister sponsored an overall Army reform bill, which the Chamber proceeded to defeat roundly.

On May 28, 1881, the Chamber voted 331 to 126 in favor of a measure that called for one year of military service in peacetime, five years in wartime, with no deferments in either case. The Senate rejected it as tantamount to an attack on private education since members of religious teaching orders were not exempt.

Swiss Hospitality

La Salette House in La Souste, Switzerland

Archier and his Council had been keeping a wary eye on these developments. They doubted that the Senate could be counted on to reverse Chamber votes indefinitely, and agreed that the time to shield the La Salette seminarians from the draft had come [Berthier, 1884:94]:

"In October 1881, following our bishop's advice, we settled a group of our young men in a quiet Swiss valley ... This house is admirably suited to serious study. It is located at La Souste, near Loèche in the Valais. It is surrounded on all sides by beautiful mountains. The residents are mostly German-speaking Catholics."

New beginnings once again called for heroism. Jean Berthier, Director of Scholastics and one-person faculty, together with the thirteen students—eight of whom had taken vows that year—divided their time and effort between philosophy and theology courses, the maintenance of a broken-down mansion and the cultivation of 59 acres of farmland. Strong arms never wanted for work. Hearty appetites were not as fortunate. Hemmed in by sheltering mountains that reminded them of home, however, they gave thanks for Switzerland's hospitality.

The fears of the La Salette superiors were indeed founded. In January 1882, during his ninety-day tenure as Prime Minister, Gambetta lent his support to a bill mandating three years of military service with no exceptions. That March, de Freycinet—in the Prime Minister's chair for the second time—called for the usual exemptions. The Left joined forces to defeat his proposal.

Financial Offensive

Dispersing the unauthorized orders proved to be a more unpopular and unwieldy task than the Republicans had anticipated. So they tailored new tactics to their anticlerical campaign. A financial offensive was quickly devised. Because their corporate nature enabled the orders to elude the charges ordinary citizens remitted to the State on the transfer of property by death, in the spring of 1884 the National Assembly revived the Accretion Tax Law of 1880, which required that, on the death of a religious, each of the houses of the institute pay a percentage on the deceased's share in the property held in common.

In early June of 1884, Archier travelled from La Salette to La Souste.

The news he brought from France was not reassuring. Berthier in turn shared his concerns about their host country's stringent antireligious statutes: "The sword of Damocles is hanging over us. Orders from Bern could drive every religious community out of Switzerland." Recent events in France had demonstrated that dead-letter laws can, in fact, resurrect on short notice. Both men cast their worries aside to savor the occasion that had brought them together. "On June 3, 1884, our Community had its greatest celebration ever," the local chronicler enthused. "The ordination of the first three priests from the Apostolic School of Our Lady of La Salette was held that day. Eight of our Scholastics were ordained to the diaconate and seventeen received minor orders." Among the new deacons was Pierre Pajot (1860-1928).

Responding in March of 1886 to Leo XIII's " conciliatory pilotage," President Grevy unexpectedly suspended the standing Army Law. Undaunted, the Chamber passed a three-year-no-exemptions bill the very next year. The Senate, predictably, voted to restore the exemptions. In 1888 a resolute Chamber enacted a three-year no exemptions bill. The Senate once more reinstated the exemptions. The deadlock appeared hopeless. As the general elections approached, however, a realistic reading of their constituents' mood pressured the Deputies to accept the Senate's terms by a 306 to 162 margin on July 8, 1889.

Momentous Decisions

Delegates to the 1891 Chapter of the La Salette Missionaries met at La Salette on May 1 through 29. A sense of destiny pervaded their gathering. Unsettling times and an uncertain future required calm heads and steady hands at the helm. Elected to a three-year term of Congregation leadership were Superior General: Auguste Chapuy (1826-1907); Assistants: Pierre Archier, Jean Berthier, and Jean-Claude Villard (1845-1907); Secretary: Célestin Thomas (1846-1900); Treasurer: Joseph Perrin (1836-1913).

The end of government interference was nowhere in sight. What havoc the National Assembly might be scattering about next no one presumed to predict. How reliable a haven for the Scholastics Switzerland, or even Italy, would prove to be was a matter of conjecture. Most capitulars agreed that conscription would hamper recruitment or interrupt the formation process and urged that it be averted if at all possible.

By grace of the Senate, military service for clerics in major orders had been reduced to one year. Neither the younger seminarians nor the Brothers qualified for exemption. As finally framed, the Army Law of 1889 prescribed that "upon completion of one year of training the following are exempt from further military duty in peacetime: teachers, committing themselves to public education for ten years; members of teaching orders, pledging ten years of service in the colonial schools of Indochina or Africa; seminarians of the established churches, if ordained to the ministry before the age of 26" [Acomb, 1967: 188].

Though it made the intent of the projected move patently clear, the historic Capitular Decision of 1891 left the destination oddly unspecified [Novel, 1968: 47]:

> "The Chapter bids the General Council attend to the establishment of a residence abroad [à l'etranger] for the purpose of safeguarding our subjects who are liable to military service."

Both a prospective foundation in the New World and a degree of hesitation are intimated here. The need to relocate the La Salette seminarians was real. The number of suitable European countries was limited. Freedom of religion was constitutionally guaranteed in Canada and the United States. The audacious Norway adventure a decade before had shown that distance, isolation, language barriers, and the Protestant ethos were surmountable obstacles. Still, questions remained. How ready a welcome could a clerical Congregation, seeking to found major and minor seminaries and engaging in the ministry mostly to support these houses of formation, expect to find in North America? Their experiences in Norway and Switzerland had proved that these Frenchmen, at least, could adapt to other European cultures. But America and Europe were two different worlds. How well would the La Salette spirituality travel across the Atlantic? [Jaouen, 1953: 132]:

> "Could children of a totally different background and culture, invited by foreign priests to follow a Weeping Virgin they themselves honored at a shrine back home, take on the spirit of La Salette?"

The disruption of their apostolic lives and plans hardly represents the full measure of the distress the Missionaries experienced. Republican exertions to strip the Church of its former prestige and curb its continued influence on society affected them at a far deeper level. These men had never ceased to champion the virtue of religion as the hallmark of La Salette spirituality.

Surely, they grieved to see the error of human self-sufficiency and the arrant exclusion of God as irrelevant to public life gain accreditation as dogmas of modernity.

Fr. Sylvain-Marie Giraud, M.S. (1830-1885), second La Salette Superior General and acclaimed Spiritual Director and author

Constant reflection on the mystery of La Salette had long since sensitized the men to the dire implications of contemporary trends. They themselves had become the quarry of repressive government measures. Displaying their customary interpretive restraint, however, they shunned the apocalyptic gloom so many were associating with apparitions in favor of a God-given hope.

Giraud, the influential La Salette spiritual master, had consistently diagnosed ills within as well as without the body of believers. Shortly after Victor Emmanuel II of Sardinia (1820-1878) had overrun the Papal States, he appended a short piece entitled "Our Lady of La Salette and the World" to his *Spiritual Exercises*. This succinct essay, traces of which have found their way into the present Rule of Life of the Missionaries of La Salette [*Constitutions* IV.23.§5], underscored the twofold evil and the twofold gift of healing the Apparition brings to light [Giraud, 1946: 386-388]:

> "I. There is an evil—and it is appalling—that ever compromises the existence, the life of our modern society. It is the spirit of independence. Here then is the Queen of heaven and earth speaking to us about submission. To whom? To God. The very notion that the remedy is to be found here escapes us nowadays.
>
> "II. There is an evil—and it too is appalling—that ever compromises the moral life, the dignity of the human person, and what is more, the eternal salvation of each one of us. It is the spirit of shallowness, the spirit of fickleness, the spirit of weakness.
>
> "Is not the Apparition of the Blessed Virgin, crowned with honor and glory, yet suffering and shedding tears, the most sublime expression of the seriousness of life and of the indispensable necessity of repentance, mortification and penance?"

"Can we fail to see that the peril is extreme?" Giraud exclaimed. But he was quick to add, quoting Wisdom 1:14 from the Vulgate: "Yet hope is to be found somewhere because 'the nations have been made curable.'" It is not astonishing then that the mounting crisis they faced in the 1890s sent Our Lady's Missionaries back to the ministry of the spoken and written word. In their own variation on St. Paul's " ... woe to me if I do not preach (the Gospel)" (1 Corinthians 9:16), they resolved again to challenge their hearers and readers to sincere conversion and unshaken allegiance to Christ.

It is the rare revolution that does not eventually betray the ideals of the revolution itself. In their zeal to bring what they considered to be an unfinished French Revolution to completion, the leaders of the Third Republic obliterated the line between society and state, fusing them together to create a "Grand Society" that might serve as the sole agent of desired change. Charges of despotism leveled against the Republic were not entirely unfounded.

Genuine democracy recognizes an order of rights that are antecedent to the state, which is not the society but rather the political form the society takes on to transact its public affairs. These are the rights of the person, the family, the churches, the associations people freely form for cultural, economic, religious and social ends. Such prior rights are no more to be violated by democratic majorities than they are by absolute monarchies. The predetermined secularizing agenda of the Third Republic strenuously promoted freedom from religion rather than freedom of religion. It rode roughshod over the antecedent right of countless citizens to form free associations for religious purposes.

What political views the men of La Salette may have privately held, what party philosophy they may have personally favored must, in the absence of extant records, remain moot questions. Their collective posture was shaped over time, though, by escalating government intolerance and the growing conviction that the State was indeed abusing its authority.

As a Community, they decided not to seek parliamentary authorization in 1880, to treat the provisions of the Accretion Tax Law of 1884 with benign neglect, and to circumvent the Compulsory Military Service Act of 1889.

For Your Reflection

Scripture: 1 Corinthians 9:16, 19-23 (I became all things to all people)

"If I preach the gospel, this is no reason for me to boast, for an obligation has been imposed on me, and woe to me if I do not preach it! ... I have made myself a slave to all so as to win over as many as possible. To the Jews I became like a Jew to win over Jews; to those under the law I became like one under the law ... to win over those under the law. To those outside the law I became like one outside the law … to win over those outside the law. To the weak I became weak, to win over the weak. I have become all things to all, to save at least some. All this I do for the sake of the gospel, so that I too may have a share in it."

Questions for reflection:

The La Salette Missionaries made sacrifices in order to follow their call to preach the good news which Mary shared with the two children at La Salette.

- What special sacrifices have you (or someone you know) made to follow God's call in life?
- Who is a person whom you admire for their openness to the needs of others?

Prayer:

Mary, Mother of the Needy, your gentle sensitivity to the two young children standing before you were most moving. You noticed their difficulty in understanding you and so you responded promptly to put them at ease. You want us to understand the good news you have brought for us to hear.

Guide us through this journey of life so that we may follow more closely to the ways and message of your Son. Through your example, make us better reflections of Jesus, our Savior and Brother.

We ask this through your loving intercession and through the grace of your Son who lives with the Father, and the Holy Spirit, one God, for ever and ever. Amen.

La Salette Invocation:

Our Lady of La Salette, Reconciler of Sinners, pray without ceasing for us who have recourse to you.

Chapter Three:
An Inviting New World

The Air of the Republic

John Ireland (1838-1918), first Archbishop of St. Paul, Minnesota and a religious and civic leader

The Fourth Centenary of the Voyage of Columbus to America distracted many weary Europeans from their own problems and struggles as it drew their attention to the New World. The more liberal-minded French clergy and laity were quite fascinated by the Church in the United States. This interest was stimulated by the visit to France in 1892 of John Ireland (1838-1918), Archbishop of St. Paul, Minnesota. Wearing a plain black cassock and speaking fluent French, he addressed a distinguished audience in the Hall of the Geographic Society in Paris on June 18 [Phillips, 1967:246]:

"The Church in America is the Church of the people. Our priests, our bishops, ... live among the people which recognizes them as its protectors and friends. We give much time to the sanctuary and the sacristy, but we give much, too, to public life. The American people likes to see the clergy occupying themselves with all the interests of the country. They feel that they are necessarily a social force. Our hearts beat always for the Republic of the United States. In the past it was said that the Catholic Church could not reconcile itself with the Republic and that the free air of the Republic would be fatal to it. The Catholic Church has breathed the air of the Republic and thrives on it very well."

What was in the air of the Republic in 1892?

Immigrants arriving at Ellis Island in New York Harbor in 1915

On January 1, Ellis Island became a receiving station for immigrants. The Republican National Convention (June 7-11) nominated President Benjamin Harrison (1833-1901) for reelection. The Democratic National Convention (June 21-23) nominated Grover Cleveland (1837-1908) for the presidency. Strained capital and labor relations erupted into violence in July. When a contract between the Amalgamated Association of Iron and Steel Workers and the Carnegie Steel Company expired, the company cut wages and refused to recognize the union. A pitched battle ensued between the 300 Pinkerton guards the company had hired to protect its plant near Pittsburgh, Pennsylvania, and the steel-workers. Three of the guards and ten of the strikers were killed.

On August 4, when her father Andrew and her stepmother Abby were found murdered by the blows of an ax in their home in Fall River, Massachusetts, suspicion fell on Lisbeth Borden (1860-1927). On September 7, James "Gentleman Jim" Corbett (1866-1933) won the first world heavyweight boxing championship by knocking out John L. Sullivan (1858-1918) in the twenty-first round.

The World's Columbian Exposition opened in Chicago on October 20. At the cost of $22,000,000, 150 acres of fairgrounds had been readied for this extravaganza. On November 8, Cleveland was elected President of the United States: 5,554,414 popular votes to Harrison's 5,190,802. The Carnegie Steel strike ended on November 20. The union was destroyed; few of the striking workers ever regained their jobs. On St. John's Day, December 27, the cornerstone of what was intended to be the largest church in America, the Episcopal Cathedral of St. John the Divine, was laid.

Looking West on Court of Honor and Grand Basin of
1893 World's Columbian Exposition in Chicago, Illinois

The First Church of Christ Scientist was founded in Boston by Mary Baker Eddy (1820-1910). The first house designed by Frank Lloyd Wright (1867-1959) was built in the Windy City. George Ferris (1859-1896) engineered the first Ferris Wheel. 250 feet high, it carried forty passengers in its thirty-six cars, and enthralled visitors to the Columbian Exposition.

Among the best-selling books of 1892 were: the final edition of *Leaves of Grass* by Walt Whitman (1819-1892); *The Quality of Mercy*, a novel by William Dean Howells (1837-1920) that probed the relationship between the economic order and personal crime; *The History of David Grieve* by Mary Augusta Ward (1851-1920), a novel promoting the social application of Christianity. *"After the Ball Is Over"* by Charles K. Harris (1865-1930) was the hit song

Borne on swelling waves of expansion and prosperity, the nation basked in euphoria at the close of the century. Describing this boom era in terms of both excitement and crisis, analysts acknowledged that a good measure of optimism was warranted but pointed to a troubled underside. Mark Twain (1835-1910) dubbed the 1890s The Gilded Age: "Glitter on the surface, but squalor beneath." The leaps and bounds of prodigious industrial growth exacted a costly toll of human misery. Seven-day workweeks, ten-hour workdays, and substandard working conditions were not uncommon. The relationship between labor and management had grown stormy. The story of the bustling cities was the saga of unskilled and underpaid immigrant labor; the all too familiar tale of human exploitation.

In a massive, unprecedented reciprocal transformation process, America was becoming the land of immigrants and the immigrants were becoming America [McManners, 1966: 391]:

> "By the end of the nineteenth century, a million Europeans were landing on the shores of the United States of America every year, and the earlier waves of the vast immigration were multiplying in their new country so that here, in potentiality, was the most powerful nation in the world. This vast, anonymous immigration had thrown up no heroes and its records are barren of dramatic incident, but its effects will be remembered long after the achievements of even the greatest nineteenth-century heads of state are forgotten."

The Church and the Age

The Church fully shared in the prevailing optimism, never doubting that it could thrive in the United States and cherishing bright dreams of apostolic success here. Between 1880 and 1900 the Catholic population doubled, rising from six to twelve million, a significant percentage of the total population, which 1890 census figures had set at 62,947,714. New dioceses were being founded nearly every year. Churches and rectories, schools and convents, homes for the aged, hospitals and orphanages—their construction costs defrayed by dint of heroic sacrifice—could not be built fast enough. Of necessity, brick and mortar topped the growing Church's agenda. An impressive transformation was again taking place [Hennesey, 1981: 5]:

> "Catholicism in the immigrant period was increasingly influenced by the needs of the newcomers, who were in fact so numerous that in a real sense they became the American Catholic Church."

Third Plenary Council of Baltimore on December 7, 1884

What the Catholic Church in the United States desired most was full acceptance as a trusted participant in the life of the country. The basic loyalty of Catholic citizens still came under attack too frequently. A Catholic population increasing at a substantially higher rate than the population at large could only fuel fears of Vatican interference in American affairs. The mother tongues they spoke, the Old-World customs they retained, lent the Church of the immigrants the look of a foreign institution. Their European roots, many suspected, would keep the latest arrivals subservient to the papacy. In the Pastoral Letter they issued at the conclusion of the Third Plenary Council of Baltimore on December 7, 1884, the Bishops of the United States had credited Americans with good sense and fair-mindedness in the matter of Catholic allegiance [Guilday, 1923: 234-235]:

"... writers and speakers who know the Church only by the caricatures drawn by prejudice, have occasionally reechoed the charge that the Catholic citizen's loyalty is exclusively to the Pope; but despite local and temporary excitements, the good sense of the American people has always prevailed against the calumny.

"We think we can claim to be acquainted both with the laws, institutions and spirit of the Catholic Church, and with the laws, institutions and spirit of our country, and we emphatically declare that there is no antagonism between them.

"We repudiate with equal earnestness the assertion that we need to lay aside any of our devotedness to our Church to be true Americans; the insinuation that we need to abate any of our love for our country's principles and institutions to be faithful Catholics."

With a keen sense of historical awareness and in language that anticipated that of Vatican Council II, a number of prominent American bishops advocated dialogue as a means of narrowing the gap between faith and science, religion and liberty, the Church and the modem world. For these men, Leo XIII's epochal Encyclical, *Rerum Novarum*, of May 15, 1891, sounded a clarion call to openness, adaptation and action in a changed and changing world. The markedly positive interpretation they attached to these "new things" reflected the climate of opportunity and optimism in which they ministered.

Nicknamed "the Midwestern Blizzard" by his fellow us, Ireland challenged the American Church in the sermon he preached on October 18, 1893, for the silver jubilee of the episcopal ordination of James Gibbons (1834-1921), Cardinal Archbishop of Baltimore [Ireland, 1897:90]:

"The Church and the age are at war. I blame the age. Elated with its material and intellectual successes, it is proud and it exaggerates its powers. In its worship of the new, it regards whatever is old with suspicion. I blame the Church. I am not afraid to say that, during the century whose sun is now setting, many leaders of thought in the Church have made the mistake of being too slow to understand the new age and too slow to extend to it the conciliatory hand of friendship. Leo has the courage of his high mission. Pope as he is, he has opponents within the Church, people whose sickly nerves suffer from the vibrations of the ship moving under his hand with accelerated velocity; reactionaries who think that all the wisdom and all the providential guidance of the Church are with the past. My whole observation of the Mines, and in particular of this memorable Columbian year, convinces me that the Church has now her season of grace in America, and I often put to myself the anxious question: Will she profit by it?"

The United States bishops had plenty to do begging for their struggling parishes, supervising their ambitious building projects, securing a reputable parochial school system, and keeping an eye on—and when possible, a hand in—local politics inasmuch as the welfare of their flock and the interests of the Church might be affected. They had gratefully welcomed Leo XIII's *Rerum Novarum*, and roundly denounced unjust treatment of workers. For the most part, however, they were only mildly interested in a speculative reordering of society or Church-sponsored social action programs. They recognized that intemperance, poverty, labor unrest, strikes and rioting represented major problems; but they considered them part of the State's purview and looked for legislative solutions.

Most members of the American hierarchy believed that the Church in this country had overcome immense obstacles to become the most vigorous manifestation of Catholicism in the world. They espoused the principle of separation of Church and State. Many believed that the United States polity was the noblest ever devised, and that it should eventually be widely adopted.

As they well knew, the Roman Curia did not share their exuberance. Their devotion to the Constitution, therefore, sought the highest endorsement, that of Leo XIII. At times, their rhetoric lent the Pope sentiments he himself never expressed, undoubtedly because they were alien to his thinking.

John Joseph Keane, who served as Bishop of Richmond, VA; first rector of the Catholic University of America in Washington, DC

The powerful orator, John Keane (1839-1918), Bishop of Richmond, Virginia, from 1878 through 1888, then first Rector of the Catholic University of America, typified this approach in a lecture he gave on the Encyclical, *Rerum Novarum* [Greeley, 1967: 160]:

"Leo XIII has laid down the law, the only law that laborers should have a just recompense for their work. He has said that Governments must protect them in their rights ... He has simply laid down the only laws of the Democracy of the age. His unbounded love for America arises from the fact that he sees here the further advance in the legitimate sphere of Democracy. He sees here a Republic which is at the same time a rebuke to the despotisms of the past and a protest to the Red Republicanism of France. He sees here the Church and the State occupying the best positions which under existing circumstances could be expected."

For Your Reflection

Scripture: Philippians 3: 7-8,14,20 (Our true home)

"Whatever gains I had, these I have come to consider a loss because of Christ. More than that, I even consider everything as a loss because of the supreme good of knowing Christ Jesus my Lord. For his sake I have accepted the loss of all things and I consider them so much rubbish, that I may gain Christ ... I continue my pursuit toward the goal, the prize of God's upward calling, in Christ Jesus ... our citizenship is in heaven, and from it we also await a savior, the Lord Jesus Christ."

Questions for reflection:

The La Salette Missionaries were initially content with remaining in their French homeland and spreading Mary's message. Yet they were open to exploring the further implications of what Mary said in her concluding words: "Make this known to all my people."

- This must have tested their trust in her message. What personal qualities are needed to move permanently to another land?

- Who in your family has immigrated to another country? What were some challenges and gifts they experienced?

Prayer:

Mary, Mother of the homeless and the foreigner, St. Paul has reminded us that this land of ours which we call home is not our true homeland. We belong to Christ, the Resurrected One and our true home is where he is, in heaven.

Help us become active members of the local community of the Church, accepting and serving others, listening and encouraging them as you have shown us during your appearance at La Salette. May we always treasure your words and example, until Jesus comes again.

We ask this through your loving intercession and through the grace of your Son who lives with the Father, and the Holy Spirit, one God, for ever and ever. Amen.

La Salette Invocation:

Our Lady of La Salette, Reconciler of Sinners, pray without ceasing for us who have recourse to you.

Chapter Four:
A Reconnaissance Mission

Mary's Emissaries

Leuk—in French, Loèche-Ville—is a municipality
in the district of Leuk in the canton of Valais in Switzerland

In early 1892, Chapuy and his Councilors carefully reviewed the information they had gathered on potential settlement sites outside of France. They briefly entertained a vague proposal calling for a foundation in Palestine and seriously considered establishing a foothold in England. Because the Loèche Scholasticate and Apostolic School were thriving, they also wondered whether it might not be advisable to remain in Switzerland and hope for the best.

By spring, the General Council had concluded that a reconnaissance mission to the Province of Quebec and several dioceses in the states of New York and New Jersey would undoubtedly be the wiser course. Pierre Pajot, the thirty-one-year-old Superior of the Shrine of Notre-Dame de l'Hermitage and an adept troubleshooter, was delegated to approach the local ordinaries in the name of the General Council, acquaint them with the nature of the Congregation's request, and negotiate the initial terms of agreement, should an invitation be extended.

Credentials and letters of introduction were readied. Arrangements were made for Pajot and his transatlantic traveling companion, Jean Ramel (1852-1918), Superior of the Residence on Rue Chanrion, to stay with the Redemptorists in Quebec City and with the Sulpicians in Montreal. As the departure date drew near, Ramel was taken ill. Joseph Vignon was pressed into service on very short notice. A grateful Pajot would often say in later years: "For all practical purposes, good Father Vignon, a veteran traveler for having served ten years as a missionary in Norway, was the leader of the expedition."

Her chosen emissaries took leave of Our Lady on her mountain that June 8. Kneeling at the spot where she had wept, they placed under her maternal protection the mission they were undertaking.

They journeyed in stages: by train to Antwerp, Belgium; by steamer to Southampton, England; by train to Liverpool, where on June 18 they boarded the *SS Labrador* of the Dominion Lines, bound for Montreal.

Born at Massieu (Isère) on August 10,

Fathers Pierre Pajot (above) and Joseph Vignon (below), the first two La Salette priests to establish a mission in North America

1860, Pajot entered the brand-new Apostolic School in Corps on the day before his sixteenth birthday. Gifted with a fine mind, he excelled in his studies. After his novitiate under Perrin, he took first vows at La Salette on November 21, 1879. He then served an apprenticeship as prefect at the Apostolic School on Rue Chanrion in Grenoble.

Connecticut State Capitol and Bushnell Park, Hartford, Connecticut, 1889; publisher: Hartford CT Board of Trade

In mid-October of 1881, he was part of the exodus of Scholastics to Loèche. Ordained to the priesthood there on December 20, 1884, he took up the duties of prefect at the Swiss Apostolic School. He was later on assigned to the holy mountain as sub-master to Perrin, whom he succeeded as novice master on July 6, 1890. In January of the following year, he was appointed Superior of the Vienne Residence; in the summer of 1891, Superior of the Shrine Community at Noiretable.

During his tenure as Superior General (1913-1926), be would be chided good-naturedly because of his fondness for America and the Americans: "Even when you are swamped with correspondence, Very Reverend Father, if a letter comes in from the United States, you not only read it eagerly but answer it instantly." "I do receive a lot of mail from over there," he would reply. "They must say to themselves: 'He knows how it is. He will understand.'"

Born at Saint-Pierre de Mésage (Isère) on April 6, 1861, Vignon enrolled at the Apostolic School in Corps in 1877. He made his first profession on the mountain of La Salette on November 21, 1879. At age nineteen, he was among the first contingent that set out for Norway during the summer of 1880.

Ordained a priest in Trondheim on August 2, 1885, he ministered in that city for five years. In 1890, he was assigned to Christiania, as Oslo was then called, where he served with loving dedication until the Missionaries of Our Lady of La Salem withdrew from Norway two years later.

"Of Father Vignon one must say that he left his heart in America," his eulogist would note in September of 1912. "Visceral ties kept him attached to that land and made of him an incorrigible optimist. His affection for America made him think that everything about it was just wonderful, and when he spoke about it—which was often—there was no end to the conviction and warmth, and enthusiasm he exuded. To the end of his days he cherished the secret desire of returning there. 'If I were allowed to go back,' he once confided to a confrere, I would very gladly crawl to the dock on my knees, if I had to.'"

The *SS Labrador* docked in Quebec on July 2. Within days Pajot and Vignon had concluded a whirlwind round of visits several dioceses in the Province of Quebec. In most instances, a record number of religious communities had recently been received, and the bishops felt that the spiritual needs of their flock were quite adequately being met. The interviews were cordial but unproductive.

This disappointing phase of their mission and the decided advantage of a common language now behind them, the legates apprehensively crossed the border into the United States on July 6. They traveled down New York state, calling on Bishops Henry Gabriels (1838-1921) of Ogdensburg, Patrick Ludden (1836-1912) of Syracuse, Francis McNeimy (1828-1894) of Albany, Archbishop Michael Corrigan (1839-1902) of New York, Bishops Charles McDonnell (1854-1921) of Brooklyn, and Winand Wigger (1841 -1901) of Newark, New Jersey.

(With or without prior appointments and given the very best train connections possible, the number of cities and bishops the men are traditionally reported to have visited in the space of a few days suggests that their itinerary has been considerably compressed in the retelling.)

Only in Ogdensburg was a tangible offer put forth. Judging its terms inadequate to the primary intent of the migration to the New World, the delegates reluctantly declined to pursue it. What they were requesting was permission to establish the minor seminary, novitiate and major seminary levels of formation in a diocese, along with the pastoral charge of a parish large enough—sufficiently affluent—to support the venture. A tall order. Gabriels' proposal that the La Salette Missionaries take on the remote St. Michael's Parish of about 200 souls in Antwerp, near Watertown, New York, fell short of the desired objective.

They had been given a sympathetic hearing everywhere, but the risk of an abortive mission was steadily mounting. Funds and spirits were running low. It had required a firm determination, bolstered no doubt by the General Council's clear instructions, to turn down the Ogdensburg proposition. Pajot and Vignon scarcely knew where to turn. In their frustration they agreed it might be best to return to Canada and make another attempt there. Presenting their request in French would be admittedly less strenuous and, especially, less chancy. A more insistent approach might also be in order.

A layover in Hartford would bring these travel-weary strangers closer than they dared dream to an offer of permanent hospitality in the United States.

City of Destiny

What follows has been narrated time and again, as befits the account of a founding event. It has been told and retold with the telescoping of events, the discrepancies in sequence, the variations in detail, and the differences in interpretation which inevitably cloak such encounters with Providence under the guise of coincidence. But then, our human knowledge seldom deals directly with bare, unadorned facts.

It relates to reality as lived and perceived by particular people in a time and place. And it comes upon it as a reality that has already been interpreted by a tradition and appropriated by a community.

Was the fateful stopover in Hartford on Friday, July 9, 1892, planned or unplanned? Had Pajot and Vignon intended or not intended to press for an audience with the Ordinary of Hartford before returning to Canada? Was Father William Harty's an accessory or essential role in gaining admission to the Hartford Diocese? Did the interview with the Bishop take place that same day or the following day?

Fr. William Harty

How quickly did the Bishop give Pajot and Vignon an answer? Did Bishop McMahon associate these Missionaries from France with young Abbé Sylvain-Marie Giraud, a fellow alumnus of the diocesan Seminary at Aix-en-Provence? Or did they, on learning that he spoke flawless French because he had studied theology at the Major Seminary of Aix, ask whether he might have known their older colleague? (In fact, McMahon was five years Giraud's junior in age, seven years younger than he in priesthood. Giraud began his theological studies at Aix in October of 1849 [Jaouen, 1985: 51] and was ordained a priest on December 17,1853. McMahon transferred to Aix from Rome's Propaganda Seminary in the fall of 1856 [O'Donnell, 1900: 167]. The two men studied theology at the same seminary, but they did not do so at the same time. Given Giraud's reputation for holiness, McMahon doubtless knew of him.)

It remains true that the way had been unexpectedly and wondrously prepared. Pajot and Vignon did meet with Bishop McMahon, and the rest is history!

In its barest essentials, this compelling story embodies the memory of a transforming experience. It describes the deep relationship to mystery in which we all stand. It evokes that dimension of our communal life where we are respondents rather than initiators, that ambience of grace in which we both move and are moved.

Bishop Lawrence Stephen McMahon (1835-1893), the fifth Bishop of Hartford, CT

As they made their way from the Hotel Hublein to the Cathedral to celebrate Mass on her feast day, Pierre Pajot and Joseph Vignon, we may be sure, beseeched Our Lady of Prodigies to direct their steps and bless their mission with success. Its twin square towers looming as a rampart of faith against the skyline of the Connecticut capital, St. Joseph's Cathedral had been consecrated just two months before, on May 8, the thirteenth anniversary of the appointment of Lawrence McMahon (1835-1893) as the fifth Bishop of Hartford.

Educated in the public schools of Boston, where his parents had settled from St. John, New Brunswick, when he was four months old, McMahon would serve in that city for two years as curate at Holy Cross Cathedral following his ordination to the priesthood in 1860. In response to the urgent appeal of its officers and men, McMahon was commissioned as a military chaplain by Governor John Andrew (1818-1867) and joined the 28th Massachusetts Regiment. He ministered almost singlehandedly to the troops as they engaged in the bloody Civil War battles of Second Bull Run, Antietam, and Fredericksburg. Days without food or rest took their toll. In a field hospital, the exhausted young priest hovered critically between life and death. He had done all that bravery and devotion can inspire, earning the encomium St. Paul bestows on a tireless worker for Christ (Philippians 2:30).

At the end of the war in 1865, a fully recovered McMahon willingly assumed the missionary pastorate of Bridgewater, East Bridgewater, Middleboro, Dartmouth, New Bedford, Martha's Vineyard and

Nantucket, Massachusetts, a sizable portion of the present Fall River Diocese, then part of the Archdiocese of Boston. Founding pastor of St. Lawrence, New Bedford, he was overjoyed to see the magnificent granite church he had erected—at the cost of $150,000—dedicated on August 10, 1871, patronal feast of both parish and pastor. When the Diocese of Providence, Rhode Island, was established in 1872, McMahon was appointed its first Vicar General, all the while retaining his pastoral duties in New Bedford: "Owing to the feeble health and frequent indisposition of the Bishop of Providence [Thomas Hendricken (1827-1886)], a large share of the administration of the affairs of the diocese fell upon Dr. McMahon" [Duggan, 1930: 170].

Eminently qualified, McMahon was promoted to the See of Hartford in 1879. He received episcopal consecration from John Williams (1822-1907), Archbishop of Boston, in the crypt (as basements of unfinished churches were then euphemistically called) of St. Joseph Cathedral on August 10, his name day. Bishop McMahon's fourteen years at the head of the Hartford Diocese coincided with a peak period of expansion and growth in the immigrant Church of the United States; he founded 48 parishes, dedicated 70 new churches, and opened 16 schools and convents. His name was destined to occupy an honored place in the American annals of the Missionaries of Our Lady of La Salette. Immodestly perhaps, they rank high among this hospitable bishop's lasting accomplishments the farsighted and welcome decision he made in their favor during the summer of 1892.

After they had offered Mass, the Rector of the Cathedral, William Harty (1845-1902), invited Pajot and Vignon to the rectory. The conversation moved, naturally enough, from a general discussion of the aggressively anticlerical politics of their native France to the particulars of their plight and the specific object of their quest. His guests' description of their projected foundation, as they fleshed it out in greater detail and with enthusiasm, struck a responsive chord in this pastoral man's heart.

Harty encouraged them to submit their request to the Bishop, pledged his own support as a member of the board of episcopal advisors, and recommended that they call on other diocesan consultors, notably John Van den Noort, pastor of St. Mary's in Putnam, and Florimund De Bruycker (1832-1903), pastor of St. Joseph's in Willimantic, to impress upon them the need to include a parish in the plans for the proposed venture. Whether these two clergymen were singled out because Harty believed they would be especially supportive of the project or because they were French-speaking Europeans is unclear.

Familiar with the Apparition at La Salette and deeply devoted to Mary as the Sorrowful Mother, Harty envisioned great long-range potential for spreading the devotion to Our Lady of Sorrows through the efforts of her Missionaries. In the shorter term, he saw bright prospects for the Chapel of Our Lady of Sorrows he had built in 1887 to serve the spiritual needs of some fifty families in the city's Parkville section. He and his assistants "had been tending to them from the Cathedral," but Harty foresaw that this cluster of Catholics would grow soon into a full-fledged parish. A jubilant Cathedral Rector arranged for Pajot and Vignon to meet with the Bishop. They resolved to try to obtain from him what they had failed to obtain elsewhere.

Interior of Shrine Church of St. Ann de Beaupré in Quebec in 1900; publisher: Canadian Pacific Co.

McMahon extended to his European visitors a gracious welcome. Impressed by his genuine kindness, they confidently presented their petition. He did not turn down their request but indicated that he would need time to mull it over. In any event, admitting a religious congregation to the diocese would require the consent of the episcopal consultors, and entrusting a parish to its care the approval of the Congregation *de Propaganda Fide*. "On several occasions McMahon invited the Fathers to share his table; and though he showed a lively interest in their project, he kept them very much in suspense" [Missionnaires de La Salette, 1893: 28].

Their spirits somewhat higher and their footsteps somewhat lighter, Pajot and Vignon boarded a New Haven & Hartford RR train for Quebec. From there they went, as hopeful but suppliant pilgrims, to the Shrine of Sainte-Anne-de-Beaupre. Shortly after their return to Montreal, a cable from the General Council in Grenoble set them on the move once again. They were to inspect firsthand 258 acres of land, six miles north east of Weatherford, Texas, 25 miles west of Fort Worth, donated by Miss Louise Zoe Delort, a Parisian devotee of Our Lady of La Salette, as a possible foundation site.

By now the wail of the whistle, the clickety-clack of the wheels and the lurching of the railway cars had become a routine accompaniment to these men's musings. A fifteen-day round-trip train journey took them from Montreal to the Lone Star State and back to Montreal. Located in an isolated, rural area at some distance from town and the railroad station, Weatherford—aside from its plentiful poultry and watermelons—had little to offer. "The thoroughly Protestant population" held out scant promise of either recruits or benefactions. To the predictable dismay of the one hundred or so Catholics who had hoped these Missionaries might settle in their midst, the delegates judged this tract of land ill-suited to the Congregation's current needs. The would-be benefactress expressed her own chagrin in a letter to Father Chapuy, the Superior General, noting that he personally would have done a better job of on-the-spot reconnoitering than Pierre Pajot, his inexperienced young lieutenant had. In closing, she chided the lot of them for their lack of being venturesome: *"Qu'on se souvienne de Christophe Colomb! [Remember Christopher Columbus!]."*

They met in Dallas with Joseph Martiniere (1841-1910), the Vicar General, who listened attentively to their story. He truly wished the newly created diocese were able to propose a mutually advantageous arrangement, he told Pajot and Vignon, but that was not practicable at the moment.

In early August they returned to Montreal, where they expected to find a message from Bishop McMahon waiting for them. Not a word. Disheartened, they decided to go back to Hartford and inquire personally into the matter.

Mission Accomplished

When they arrived there on August 11, McMahon allayed all their fears. He had indeed written to them several times, he assured them; his letters had obviously strayed. Knowing from experience that the night always seems darkest just before dawn, he delighted to inform them that he had taken their project to heart and reached a favorable decision. The Board of Consultors would be meeting that very day to consider the admission of the Missionaries of Our Lady of La Salette into the Diocese of Hartford.

The exultant envoys learned the next day that the Bishop's Councilors had given the proposal their unanimous endorsement. Their anxious efforts had been crowned with success; their fervent prayers had been answered.

Adding to the joy of the occasion, McMahon stated that he intended, in due time and with the concurrence of the *Propaganda Fide* Congregation, to confide a parish to the care of the Institute. And in a touching gesture that bespoke a bonding between the Diocese and the Congregation, he made the offer of the former episcopal manse on Collins Street, the McFarland Residence, named for Francis McFarland (1819-1874), the third Bishop of Hartford, who had lived there from 1872 until his death.

The good news was cabled without delay to Chapuy in Grenoble. As it spread, this word from America generated its full measure of elation. A new day had dawned for Our Lady's Missionaries. Given its legacy of bitter and unresolved Church-State conflict, France's revolutionary past would go on intruding on the present, clouding the future of all religious orders there. A succinct and telling expression of the Community's reaction to the New World foundation found its way into the *Annales* a bit later [Missionnaires de La Salette, 1893: 28]: "The future, the future is ours,' would we say, if we felt less unworthy of this opportunity."

A series of sharp dislocations would inevitably follow upon the elation. New chapters of La Salette's Book of Exodus were written by the successive expatriate contingents who left France for New York via Cherbourg, or Switzerland for New York via Antwerp on September 3, November 12, November 19, 1892; January 23, 1893 ... Acculturation, inculturation, multiculturalism—idioms familiar to our age of sociological sophistication—would have sounded as foreign to the ears of our emigrating colleagues as the oftentimes idiosyncratic English terms that puzzled them in Connecticut. Ostensibly, the decision to migrate was a temporary measure, designed to safeguard "our subjects who are liable to military service" for such time as might be necessary. Few, if any, of those assigned to Hartford in the late 1890s, however, were unaware that a permanent New World implantation was in the making.

They took sad leave of confreres, parents, family, friends, neighbors, hometown and homeland; they bade them tearful adieu in the missionary tradition of the Church and of the Congregation, in the spirit of sacrifice. They sensed that, with time and by the grace of God, they would manage to adapt to strange surroundings, gradually shed those characteristics that marked them as foreigners, learn the language of their adoptive land, and progressively take on its ways. Dared they imagine the day would come when they might think of themselves simply as Americans? By any name, the uprooting, transplanting and rerooting process had to be a wrenching experience [Missionnaires de La Salette, 1902: 57]:

> "The monastery, it seemed, had been turned into a real coffin factory. All you could hear anywhere was the pounding of

a hammer or the rasping of a saw. In a little while, a wagon pulls up, carts off a few packing crates or a few steamer trunks. You then see two or three Missionaries, surrounded by a group of young Scholastics, walking slowly and silently toward the site of the Apparition, bursting into sobs there at the feet of this Mother they love so much, trying to resign themselves to the prospect of leaving her perhaps forever. Yet they must, after all, tear themselves away. Brokenhearted and in tears, like the Virgin of the ravine, they make their way down the road from Gargas."

This latest missionary enterprise appealed to the adventurous spirit of the La Salette Apostolics, however. While struggling with the conjugation of Latin verbs and later with the intricacies of scansion, they would hear from time to time about a new foundation overseas in a place called Hartford, Connecticut, U. S. A. The whispered word among these young schoolmates was that, after their novitiate year, they would all be going over there to America to study philosophy and theology, because "despite the heroic conciliating efforts expended by Leo XIII, the government in France persisted in placing discriminatory burdens on the Church and on religious organizations in particular." This would mean saying goodbye to family and friends, maybe forever; but it would be exciting.

For Your Reflection

Scripture: James 1:2-5,12 (Perseverance in trial)

"Consider it all joy ... when you encounter various trials, for you know that the testing of your faith produces perseverance. And let perseverance be perfect, so that you may be perfect and complete, lacking in nothing. But if any of you lacks wisdom, (they) should ask God who gives to all generously and ungrudgingly, and (they) will be given it ... Blessed is the person who perseveres ... for when he has been proved he will receive the crown of life that (God) promised to those who love him."

Questions for reflection:

As the La Salette Missionaries made their many initial attempts to establish a home mission in North America, their efforts were thwarted repeatedly. Yet they persisted and were finally received with open arms into the Diocese of Hartford, Connecticut.

- What in your life (or that of others) has necessitated determination or perseverance?

- Whom do you know who has persisted in helping another in need?

Prayer:

Mary, Persistent Mother of all, in the wedding in Cana of Galilee you persisted in helping the newly married couple by asking your Son and then telling the servants to "do what he tells you."

Help us to become more like you in your loving persistence. May we never lose heart when difficulties arise. Let your loving kindness wash over us and seep into our lives in most wondrous ways. Assist us to persevere in loving others as you so generously love us today.

We ask this through your loving intercession and through the grace of your Son who lives with the Father, and the Holy Spirit, one God, for ever and ever. Amen.

La Salette Invocation:

Our Lady of La Salette, Reconciler of Sinners, pray without ceasing for us who have recourse to you.

La Salette's first home in U.S. on Collins Street in Hartford, CT, 1892, the former McFarland Residence and former Episcopal Residence

Chapter Five:
A New Beginning

Newcomers to America

The temporary quarters placed at their disposal had been vacant for some time and were in a state of considerable disrepair. To the obvious relief of Pajot and Vignon, and of their depleted purse, the roof was salvageable. Harty's assistance proved invaluable in finding laborers and the $700.00 needed to replace all the gutters. Basic food and clothing needs in the early days, the Sisters at Mount St. Joseph on Farmington Avenue, the local clergy, and kindhearted lay people generously met. A welcome the newcomers to these shores would not soon forget.

At the close of 1892, the pioneer La Salette Community in America numbered fourteen members: Fathers Pierre Pajot, Superior; Joseph Vignon, Treasurer; Jean-Pierre Guinet (1866-1923), ordained in Loèche on June 22, 1890; Clement Moussier (1860-1919), ordained in Loèche on May 31, 1886; and Pierre Roux (1864-1934), ordained in Sion on December 21, 1887; Brother Joseph Cuny, cook; Scholastics Joseph Bachelin, François Gerboud (1871-1959), Julien Ginet (1872-1949), Emile Plattier (1872-1949) and Louis Sorrel (1872-1919); Novices Etienne Xavier Cruveiller (1874-1945), Henri Galvin (1874-1962), and Constant Glatigny (1873-1905).

Letters the eighteen-year old Galvin sent home to France shortly after his arrival in the United States—circulated in mimeographed translation much later on as *Reminiscences*—offer candid sketches of student life at the comer of Collins and Woodland Streets: "... a worn-out staircase, its banister still glossy and shiny (a reminder that in years gone by this had been a fine house), led us to the second floor. The largest room up there served as our study hall and what, in the days of the former bishops must have been a chapel, had become our dormitory. Nobody had lived there for over a decade. So, it is not

Row one from left: Etienne Xavier Cruveiller (1874-1945), Henri Galvin (1874-1962), and François Gerboud (1871-1959): Row two from left: Julien Ginet (1872-1949), Hippolyte Girard (1853-1943), and Clement Moussier (1860-1919): Row three from left: Pierre Roux (1864-1934), Louis Sorrel (1872-1919), and Camille Triquet (1865-1926)

surprising that walls and ceilings were rather dilapidated. Despite the shabby appearances, health and vigor, joy and mirth reigned among all the Fathers and students in that house. We felt we were working more closely united with our Lord in his poor house at Nazareth and were truly contented and happy. ... Whenever we went out, we drew curious stares and strange smiles. We would ask one another: 'Why in the world are these people looking at us?' Our shoes bore a very distinctive foreign mark. Without our realizing it, the seven or eight of us in our hobnailed boots were making as much noise on the flagstone sidewalks as Lafayette's cavalry, charging for the freedom of the country."

In February and March of 1893, the Fathers conducted Lenten missions in French at Our Lady of the Rosary in Jewett City, at St. Edward in Stafford Springs, and at Sacred Heart in Wauregan. Preaching the La Salette message in American parishes afforded them the double satisfaction of exercising the Congregation's proper charism and of supplementing the modest income they had been earning through weekend ministry. The implantation of the Institute in the United States was officially underway; an important step toward financial self-sufficiency had also been taken.

Steady arrivals from France added significantly to the number of priests: Hippolyte Girard (1853-1943), Jules Morard (1867-1954), Clovis Socquet (1867-1917), and Camille Triquet (1865-1926).

The Scholastics Cruveiller, Galvin and Glatigny, who had begun their novitiate in France and completed it in Hartford, were professed on August 15, 1893. The vow ceremony was held in the main floor chapel of the McFarland Residence. Joseph Charles, Paul Magnat (1875-1899), Marius Michel (1874-1960), and Joseph Moussier (1873-1929) took their first vows that same day in the Basilica at La Salette. (They set out for New York and Hartford from Le Havre on September 23.)

Less than a week later, on August 21, the fledgling Community joined the faithful of the Diocese of Hartford in mourning the unexpected death of their beloved Bishop. The untimely passing of their benefactor saddened and unsettled Our Lady's Missionaries. They had been admitted to the diocese on a trial basis. The McFarland Residence would be overcrowded in no time. Construction plans should include the Apostolic School that had been part of the Hartford project from the outset. Would his successor be as sympathetic as McMahon had

First Church of Our Lady of Sorrows in the Parkville section of Hartford, CT

been? Could he be expected to grant the necessary permission as readily as McMahon?

Michael Tierney (1839-1908), Pastor of St. Mary's in New Britain, Connecticut, was consecrated the sixth Bishop of Hartford on February 22, 1894. Shortly afterwards, Pajot arranged to meet with him. Tierney gave him a warm welcome and showed genuine interest in the hopes the men were entertaining for the near future. He could only be pleased to note that the candidates for the missionary priesthood had already outgrown the accommodations on Collins Street, and went on to say: "I have a proposition to make that will, I believe, solve the problem to your best advantage. I am referring to the small suburb called Parkville in the southwest part of Hartford, where our good Father Harty has built a beautiful little church. Near that mission chapel there is a ten-acre lot that can be purchased on very approachable terms. If you could buy this land and, in view of both the present and the future, build a college for your seminarians there,

I would gladly entrust the care of the mission church to your men. In my estimation, Parkville will soon become part of the city and Our Lady of Sorrows will develop into a large parish."

Vignon spent July 3 through 15 in France, giving Chapuy and the General Council a vibrant firsthand report on the exceptional progress of the Hartford foundation to date. To keep subscribers and donors in France abreast of these promising developments, the *Annales* featured a regular column entitled, "A Letter from One of Our Americans." The authors of these initialed pieces drew comparisons, shared impressions, described ministerial activities, outlined future projects, and appealed to the continued support of their French readers [Missionnaires de La Salette, 1894:26]:

> "We gave a two-week mission in Putnam just before Easter. When we conduct missions here, we do not have to go out looking for people as we do in France...

> "We preached the teachings of the Blessed Virgin at La Salette. How attentively our dear Canadians listened to the various details of the Apparition! A few days after the mission, the young women of the parish formed a musical society, which they chose to call Our Lady of La Salette Circle. Recently, they presented the Apparition in a series of tableaux. The scene of the Virgin speaking with the children was particularly effective. We shall soon be doing here in America what is not being done in France in honor of the Virgin of the Alps. What we could not do if we had sufficient resources to represent the Apparition in life-size statuary! The land was bought, but it is not paid for."

A letter of this type described in some detail the well-attended October 7, 1894, cornerstone blessing ceremony on New Park Avenue. In a parenthetical and semi-apologetic comment, the French editor points up a telltale sign of incipient Americanization [Missionnaires de La Salette, 1894: 109]: "The Fathers had the excellent idea of distributing a little English leaflet on the Apparition during the ceremony (a somewhat American approach, but a very practical means, you will admit, of making our divine Mother's admonitions known to all)."

St. Joseph's Church in Fitchburg, Massachusetts from an early postcard

Contrary to the earliest expectations, the Diocese of Springfield, rather than Hartford, would be the first to confide a parish to the Institute. On October 11, 1894, the Missionaries of La Salette took official charge of St. Joseph's Parish in Fitchburg, Massachusetts. Vignon was appointed pastor; Girard, Roux and Triquet, assistants. A flare-up of nationalist sentiment greeted them on arrival, but it soon subsided: "The Canadians sulked at first, then came around" [Rumilly, 1965: 152].

Thanks to Harty's guiding influence and patient nurture, Our Lady of Sorrows simultaneously attained parochial status and passed into the hands of Our Lady's Missionaries on Ascension Thursday, May 23, 1895. To Guinet, his genial successor and the parish's first canonical pastor, Harty bequeathed a debt-free church and a spirited congregation of 120 families.

In the presence of numerous invited guests and of this impressive $45,000 structure's awed denizens, the 114 by 45 foot La Salette College received the solemn blessing of the Bishop of Hartford on September 19,1895, the forty-ninth anniversary of the Apparition. On November 16 through 22, it hosted the Community's first canon-

La Salette College Seminary, New Park Avenue, Hartford, CT; original building before expansion; perhaps early 1900s

St. James Parish in Danielson, CT; from left: Rectory, Church and Convent

ical visitor, the General Councilor Villard. Its two newest members: Jean Pilloix (1877-1932), professed on October 27, 1895, and Jean Roux (1878-1963), professed on June 21, 1895, had crossed the Atlantic with him.

In his capacity as Visitator, Villard called on the local Ordinary. Among other matters, the Congregation's willingness to take on St. James Parish in Danielson, Connecticut, was discussed at length. Tierney quite frankly admitted that Danielson, a hotbed of French-Canadian agitation, would pose a real challenge. A reconciler's finest hour.

Before the year ended, the restive Danielson parish had come under the pastoral care of Our Lady's Missionaries. Clovis Socquet was called to serve as its first La Salette pastor.

Saga of Danielson

Socquet stepped into a hornet's nest. In one of the numerous episodes of the nationalist crisis that rocked the Church in the closing decades of the last century, the people of Danielson had been feuding with their bishop and their pastor for several years.

The mass of Catholic laity—having little education and toiling to make ends meet in a new world—took no interest or part in the debates that vexed the theologians and divided the hierarchy. Scant few laypeople, however, were not emotionally involved in the nationalities controversy.

French-Canadian immigrants had come to the mill towns of New England laden with a history of ethnic controversy. Dominance by the English-speaking majority of Canadians members of the Church of England, for the most part—had fostered a siege mentality in the French-speaking and Roman Catholic Province of Quebec [Perko, 1989: 149]: "For generations, the Church had served not only as a religious institution but as a vehicle for the preservation of a threatened language and culture. For French-Canadians, the Church was a bulwark of their ethnic heritage as well as of their faith."

Taking their parish priest, Thomas Preston, at his word, the French-Canadians in Danielson had contributed generously to the building-fund drive with the understanding that the parochial school would offer a bilingual curriculum. Once the school opened in 1889, the promise was forgotten. A committee of concerned parishioners drafted a petition requesting more hours of French in the classroom. An angry majority eagerly signed it; Preston took it under advisement.

Charles Leclaire, M.D., a prominent member of the congregation by reason of the respected profession he practiced and the outspoken patriotism he professed, spearheaded a movement for redress. Any who tangled with "the Lion of Danielson" found him to be a tenacious adversary.

In 1892, their patience with Preston's inaction at an end, several irate parishioners drew up a second petition, calling for more French in the school and demanding the appointment of a French-Canadian pastor. Leclaire personally delivered this petition to McMahon. The Bishop responded by naming Arthur Dusablon, a priest of the Archdiocese of Montreal, curate in Danielson. Though sympathetic to the grievances of his compatriots, as an interloper at St. James, Dusablon was in no position to resolve them. Two years later, he returned in frustration to the relative tranquility of his home diocese.

In June of 1894, Leclaire presented his respects and the Danielson petition to the new Bishop of Hartford. Tierney counseled patience. Reporting on the interview and its disappointing outcome, *L'Opinion Publique*—part of the watchdog nationalist press network—commented [Rumilly, 1965: 150]: "In its desire to denationalize the French-Canadian element, the rage for assimilation does not hesitate to sacrifice the quality of religious service."

The controversy then took an ugly turn. A derogatory remark, allegedly made by Preston, about the size of French-Canadian families was bruited about as an instance of the low esteem in which Canadians were held by the clergy. Adding fuel to the fire, the Belgian-born De Bruycker of Willimantic branded the Danielson dissenters "rebels and socialists."

Leclaire and his associates decided to refer the matter to Archbishop Francesco Satolli (1839-1910), Apostolic Delegate to the United States. The Danielson envoys were given short shrift in Washington. The Archbishop advised his Connecticut supplicants that they were at fault and bore a grave responsibility for troubling the harmony of the Church.

In June of 1895, the committee called a strike. A significant number of parishioners stayed away from church. Appalled, J. E. Bourret, the pastor of St. Anne's in Waterbury, resolved to make an attempt at mediation. He emerged from his long meeting with Tierney bearing a hopeful message for the disgruntled ones of Danielson [Rumilly, 1965: 151]: "Submit, and within two months you will have a French-Canadian pastor. Our Bishop has gone so far as to specifically mention Father Paul Eugene Roy (Bishop, d. February 20, 1926), the pastor of St. Anne's in Hartford." The strike ended immediately, and the truant parishioners returned to church. As their spokesman, Leclaire pledged that "the recalcitrant would henceforth be meek and submissive as lambs." Two months elapsed; Preston remained at the helm. A meeting was called; the word strike was spoken once more.

Two of the parishioners, Moïse Bessette and Eloi Jette, were delegated to discuss the Danielson impasse with Tierney. In his conversation with them on October 8, the Bishop indicated that a change could be expected soon [Rumilly, 69 1965: 152]: "'A year from now, Excellency? Six months from now?' They pressed him. He replied: 'A year would be too long to wait.'" Thomas Preston, the pastor there for twelve years, departed Danielson on December 3. Enter Clovis Socquet.

Stunned by this episcopal sleight of hand, many parishioners voiced acute displeasure and vowed they would not back down [Rumilly, 1965: 152]: "We are not a tribe of Indians that we should be ministered to by foreign priests. Europeans —be they French-speaking Belgians, Swiss or Frenchmen from France—do not know our customs, aspirations, and needs; all things considered, they are not a whole lot better than the Irish pastors." In a blatant display of prejudice, *L'Opinion Publique* offered this observation [Rumilly, 1965: 153]: "Our new pastor made a magnificent first impression, and it is unfortunate that he is not Canadian."

"What particularly enraged them as the battle continued was that Bishop Tierney's solution was to commission two religious congregations from France (the La Salette Fathers and the Sisters of Saint Joseph of Chambery) to address the language problem properly. It was a reaction that dumbfounded Tierney; equally shocked were the apostolic delegate and Roman officials, who understood the goodwill behind the bishop's move" [Liptak, 1989: 167].

With the withholding of pew rent, the protest entered a new phase in early 1896. *La Tribune* of Woonsocket, Rhode Island, applauded the boycott and reaffirmed the validity of the cause [Rumilly, 1965: 153]: "What ours want is a priest of their own tongue, blood, race. It is their right." On January 4, James Healy (1830-1900), Bishop of Portland, who had always shown the French-Canadians of his Maine diocese every consideration and who had also learned how exacting and exasperating they could be, sent Tierney a brief note, advising: "Stand to your guns and let them rave" [Liptak, 1989: 165].

A number of concerned clergy—labeled assimilationists for their trouble—cautioned their compatriots against putting ethnicity before catholicity. These same priests also appealed to the Apostolic Delegate, hoping that Tierney might be persuaded to make some concessions, however minor. Satolli chose to tar conciliators and hotheads with the same brush: "This agitation is entirely unwarranted. The provision made by the Bishop for the spiritual needs of his flock is more than adequate."

A fresh outburst followed Socquet's refusal to baptize a "rebel" couple's child. On March 31, the Apostolic Delegate heard from Danielson once again. In his April 27 reply to Leclaire, he wrote [Rumilly, 1965: 154]: "I am aware of what has been done to provide you with a priest who can certainly meet all your needs as French-speaking parishioners since he himself is French. Your obstinacy can only serve to cast suspicion on your good faith and to suggest that you are pursuing an objective other than that which your complaint sets forth. If you really seek your religious welfare and that of your children, it is your duty to behave like good Catholics and submit to the governance of your Bishop, who has dealt with you in a most paternal spirit." Some parishioners desisted. The majority remained in Leclaire's camp.

Welcoming the opportunity to abet their complete break with the Roman Catholic Church and swell the ranks of his own sect, Joseph René Vilatte (1854-1929), Archbishop of renegade French Catholics in Wisconsin, dispatched envoys to the resisters in Danielson. Thwarted—so they insisted—by their Bishop, scolded by the Apostolic Delegate, and courted at this point by schismatics, the parishioners of St. James were in a rare predicament.

The climate remained unremittingly tense. It is with some trepidation that the twenty-nine-year-old pastor of St. James anticipated the election of parish wardens in early 1897. "By statute of the State of Connecticut, the financial interests of each parish rest in the hands of a corporation ... made up of the Bishop of the diocese, the Vicar General of the diocese, the pastor of the parish and two laymen of the parish who are known as trustees. The laymen are elected annually in January" [Duggan, 1930: 204]. To preclude infiltration by Leclaire's partisans, Socquet not only presided at the corporation meeting and served as recording secretary; he also made and seconded all the motions. The election was contested. A civil suit was filed.

Interior of St. James Church in Danielson, CT in 1917

Ghetto of Ghettos

In its ethnic unrest, Danielson did not stand alone. Catholic dioceses throughout the country were seamed by segregation along national lines. Parochialism at its worst had everywhere taken on a combative and defensive stance. This internal strife was, at times, as alarming as it was disedifying: "A ghetto of ghettos, we might call this cluster of officially united yet practically diverse and divided set of peoples ... There were more reasons for Catholic Irish to fight Catholic Germans, and more satisfying ones for Catholic Poles to fight other Catholic Poles than to be distracted by buzzing, biting Protestants" [Marty, 1986: 130-131].

Surveying the minefield, the Vatican's first tendency was to maintain a neutral posture. As Mariano Rampolla (1843-1913), the Cardinal Secretary of State, expressed it to Denis O'Connell (1849-1927), Rector of the North American College in Rome: "Unfortunately, there are two parties in the United States and the Holy See cannot favor either of them" [Letter of January 17, 1891. *Baltimore Cathedral Archives*, 88-H-2]. In July of that same year he wrote to Gibbons: "The Head of the Church Universal is not inclined to provoke even the slightest misgivings and urges Your Eminence to work together with his brother bishops for the restoration of peace" [Moynihan, 1953: 68].

When conferring the pallium on Frederick Katzer (1844-1903), the Austrian-born Archbishop of Milwaukee whose transfer to that see from Green Bay in January of 1891 had produced its share of flak, Gibbons translated this advice into an appeal for a Church unity that would overcome divisions and transcend nationalities [Will, 1922: 528]:

> "Woe to those, beloved, who would destroy or impair this blessed harmony that reigns among us! Woe to those who would sow the tares of discord in the fair fields of the Church in America! ... Brothers and sisters we are, whatever our nationality may be, and brothers and sisters we shall remain. We will prove to our fellow citizens that the ties formed by grace and faith are stronger than flesh and blood. Loyalty to

God's Church and to our country! This is our religious and political faith. Let us glory in the title of American citizens. We owe our allegiance to one country, and that country is America."

The merest suggestion that anything foreign attached to the Church in the United States galled the majority of its bishops. Ireland of St. Paul was decidedly among them: "As far as the Church's garments assume color from the local atmosphere, she must be American. Let no one dare paint her brow with a foreign tint or pin to her mantle foreign linings." John Lancaster Spalding (1840-1916), Bishop of Peoria, Illinois, was one of the rare progressives to break ranks on the question of assimilation [Greeley, 1967: 168]: "From whatever part of the world they come immigrants have the right," he emphasized, "to maintain their customs, languages, religious practices."

Church leaders agreed that immigrant Catholics should adapt to the ways of their adoptive land, aspire to responsible United States citizenship, and gain their rightful place in the mainstream of American life. Differences of opinion arose over the pace of these adjustments: a sharp break with Old World customs, languages and traditions from the outset, or a gradual process of assimilation over time, encompassing successive generations.

A more fundamental difference of opinion arose over the kind of adjustment to be made. Convinced as they were that the Catholic experience in the United States held worldwide significance, liberal Churchmen thought the social and political order in America embodied genuine values neither implemented nor fully appreciated by Europeans, including members of the Roman Curia.

In their view, the times posed a crucial question: "Will the modern world influence the traditional faith, or will the traditional faith influence the modern world?" With the optimism that characterized the 1890s, they concluded that the old faith had nothing to fear from political and religious freedom. From this platform they deprecated anything that created, or appeared to create, unnecessary opposition between the Church and American culture.

Conservative Churchmen, on the other hand, gave more attention to those aspects of American culture that they considered irreconcilable with Catholicism: the growing agnosticism of contemporary thinkers, the blatant materialism of American society, the profit-crazed basis of industrial expansion, the creeping secularization of the public-school system and the overt hostility of the Protestant majority to Roman Catholicism.

To the assimilationists, Franco-Americans, German-Americans, Italo-Americans, Polish-Americans, ... constituted an anomaly. To the nationalists, these very hyphenated Catholics, clinging to the faith and family values of their respective countries of origin, constituted a bulwark against encroaching secularism.

Neither side in the debate entirely resisted excess. Forced assimilation misread the complexity of the process and underestimated the time factor it involved. Pressured Americanization, more often than not, proved to be counterproductive. Attacks on their ethnic traits and the denial of their rights could only reinforce the immigrants' nationalist group identity and estrange them from the wider Church. By the same token, a narrow and exclusive focus on nationalist concerns could only breed chauvinism and a particularism unbecoming a universal Church.

At the height of the nationalities controversy, ethnic interest groups besieged Rome with urgent appeals and requests. To cite but a few examples: In 1887, forty-three French priests of the archdiocese forwarded a petition to Miss Lucie Faure, daughter of Félix Faure (1841-1899), President of the Third Republic, asking that she use her influence at the Vatican to obtain the nomination of a Frenchman as Archbishop of New Orleans. Their efforts were foiled. Francis Janssens (1843-1897), the Dutch-born Rector of the Cathedral in Richmond, Virginia, was chosen. Honoré Mercier (1840-1894), the Prime

This Franco-American flag, on July 24th 2012, was made the official Franco-American Day in the states of Connecticut, Maine, New Hampshire, and Vermont.

Minister of Quebec, rushed to Rome in 1891 to urge the appointment of Canadian bishops in the New England states. Polish priests in Chicago insisted that immigrant Poles be given bishops selected from among their own ranks. They enlisted the good offices of none other than President Grover Cleveland in pleading their cause in Rome.

The Vatican had little choice but to take a stand. In May of 1892, Mieceslaus Ledochowski (1822-1902), Cardinal Prefect of the Propaganda Congregation, forwarded to the United States hierarchy a message that was known to articulate the personal views of Leo XIII [Moynihan, 1953: 69-70]:

> "Whenever an episcopal see is vacant in America, clergy and people become excited, different factions discuss possible candidates in meetings and, through the public press, seek by all means to advance their favorites. The chief cause of these divisions is that Catholics, dividing on national lines, demand bishops from the ranks of their several nationalities, instead of keeping solely in view the welfare of the Church. This welfare is the sole guide of the Holy See in naming bishops for all countries, and especially must the principle be followed in the case of the United States, whither populations go from various European countries, to the end that they build up there for themselves a new "patria," where they must coalesce into one people and form together one nation."

Mieczysław Halka-Ledóchowski (1822-1902) from Poland, the Cardinal Prefect of the Propaganda Congregation

The message was clear. American Catholics were to put their ethnic divisions behind them and "coalesce into one people." The dread melting-pot principle had found its way into a curial directive. Most immigrants went on believing that it was possible in the New World to constitute a distinctive cultural-religious community that would at the same time be thoroughly American. "Polish, French, and Italian Catholics would continue to resent the domination of the Church by the Irish hierarchy, and the Irish hierarchy, clergy and laity would continue to resent the separatism and what they took to be the anti-Americanism of the immigrants ... Although it may be possible to develop some theory in which ethnic pluralism and national unity can both be protected, the practical application of such a theory escaped the Church in the 1890s and still escapes it" [Greeley, 1967: 193].

Any retrospective assessment of the reconciliation efforts put forth during the crisis by the clergy, generally, and by Clovis Socquet and his curates, Pierre Roux and Joseph Deschaux-Blanc (1866-1921), specifically, must consider the dramatic shift in consciousness that has taken place since. The contemporary concern to empower minorities, the relatively new sensitivity to minority cultures, and the growing awareness that multiculturalism is a healthy expression of equality as well as of diversity serve only to highlight the psychological and sociological ramifications of the perennial unity-in-diversity challenge.

As the period of confrontation waned and the traces of acrimony subsided, American church leaders began to perceive the more positive dimensions of multicultural distinctiveness. "The significance given to the parish, the respect for the gift of pastoral care, the understanding of the value of solidarity attained through Catholic organization—their insistence upon these particular aspects of their faithfulness was the outstanding legacy of French-Canadians to Catholicism in the United States" [Liptak., 1989: 170].

"Never think you've seen the last of anything"—Eudora Welty's aphorism from *The Optimist's Daughter*—surely applies here. Signs of the times: a front-page headline in the June 21, 1991, issue of The New York Times, "Panel on Schools Urges Emphasizing Minority Cultures," and a July 8, 1991, *Time* cover Story, "Whose America?" with a menacing subtitle: "A growing emphasis on the nation's 'multicultural' heritage exalts racial and ethnic pride at the expense of social cohesion."

"To do justice to these complexities intellectually—to say nothing of devising practical policies to deal with them—we must take seriously the claims of all the groups involved. No one's position should be dismissed out of hand merely by giving it an invidious label—calling it 'ethnocentric,' let us say, or dubbing it 'a product of melting-pot thinking.' We must pass beyond the shibboleths not just of Americanism, but also of pluralism" [Gleason, 1989: 57].

For Your Reflection

Scripture: 2 Corinthians 5:17-20 and 6:1 (You are a new creation)

"So whoever is in Christ is a new creation: the old things have passed away; behold, new things have come. And all this is from God, who has reconciled us to himself through Christ and given us the ministry of reconciliation, namely, God was reconciling the world to himself in Christ, not counting their trespasses against them and entrusting to us the message of reconciliation. So we are ambassadors for Christ, as if God were appealing through us. We implore you on behalf of Christ, be reconciled to God … Working together, then, we appeal to you not to receive the grace of God in vain."

Questions for reflection:

Concerning the struggles of the La Salette Missionaries to begin their new life and ministry of reconciliation in North America, we hear about the challenges of ministering *among* and *with* various cultural and ethnic groups. Yet the La Salettes pushed on, dealing directly and lovingly with opposition and maintaining a clear vision of their ministry of reconciliation "to all her people."

- When have you or others dealt well with differing opinions and troublesome conflicts?

- Do you know a person who has successfully dealt with or kept listening to another person with a differing point of view?

Prayer:

Mary, Mother of Reconciliation, in the scriptures we find examples of the differences of opinion even among the Holy Family of Nazareth, such as your expression of frustration with your young Son as he remained in the temple in Jerusalem, listening to the teachers and asking them questions. You opened your mind to his words and pondered these things in your heart, as we are called to do.

Teach us how to ponder some situations in our heart, allowing God to guide us and help us to be made anew by understanding how to deal with the challenges of life with hope and trust in the Father.

We ask this through your loving intercession and through the grace of your Son who lives with the Father, and the Holy Spirit, one God, for ever and ever. Amen.

La Salette Invocation:

Our Lady of La Salette, Reconciler of Sinners, pray without ceasing for us who have recourse to you.

Chapter Six:
A Time for Everything

A Time for Gathering

In 1897 the students of St. Joseph School in Corps, France, walked on holiday together to the source of the nearby Gillarde River

The Institute had entered an exhilarating period of expansion and diversification. By all accounts, the General Chapter that assembled in Grenoble from October 5 through November 15, 1897, consciously engaged in a two-pronged effort: to inventory and appropriate the rich diversity and to ensure that the vital center would hold, steady and strong. This concern to establish and maintain a sound equilibrium between the gratifying outward movement that was opening new opportunities in several directions and the essential inward movement that would keep the spreading Institute attached to its original inspiration marked the agenda.

Taking part in these deliberations that would set the Congregation's course for some time to come were sixteen Chapter Delegates; eight of whom were *ex officio* members: Chapuy, the outgoing Superior General; Archier, Berthier, Perrin, and Villard, the General Assistants; Thomas, the Secretary General; Auguste Ploussu (1848-1920), the Treasurer General; and Louis Beaup (1861-1936), the Master of Novices; eight of whom were elected representatives: France: Joseph Brissaud (1835-1903), St. Joseph in Corps; Isidore Burille (1856-1925), Grenoble; Casimir Gachet (1864-1941), Noiretable; Pierre Liaud (1865-1930), Grenoble; François Pra (1863-1918), Grenoble; Rome: Auguste Blache (1861-1936); and U.S.A.: Pierre Pajot and Joseph Vignon.

Revision of the Rule for presentation to the Holy See, a seemingly endless task, was on the agenda. The General Customary also stood in need of recasting. The principle of unity in diversity presided over this twofold revision.

The universal mission and purpose of the Institute, the Church-sanctioned means toward achieving these shared goals, the religious regularity to be observed by all, the common prayers and devotional practices to be carried out everywhere, and a centralized government model addressed the need for unity in essentials.

Modifications, and even mitigations, in the matter of the daily horarium, religious attire, etc., to accommodate the various apostolates, the climate, culture and customs of a specific country addressed the need to respect diversity. Adaptations of this nature would find their way into regional and local directories.

To enhance its distinctiveness and promote its unity worldwide, it was then proposed that—with ecclesiastical approval—a liturgical calendar proper to the Institute be adopted and that a La Salette ordo be published annually. The proposal carried handily.

The Chapter further devised an official communications network, designating for each of the residences an official correspondent for the *Annales*.

As part of the Thomist Revival he had launched in 1879, Leo XIII urged that religious families enroll their major seminarians at Rome's pontifical universities. Our Lady's Missionaries heeded the papal summons in 1896, at which time the Loèche residence in Switzerland closed its doors after fifteen years. Eighteen Scholastics—thirteen of whom would persevere—had in the years since 1892 sailed to the United States to pursue their studies in philosophy and theology in Hartford. Sixteen Scholastics—twelve of whom would go on to the La Salette Missionary priesthood—were sent to study in the Eternal City.

First La Salette Seminary in Rome was the residence of the Philosophy and Theology students from many countries.

Uncomfortable with the offhandedness that had characterized the Community's approach to education over the years, several Delegates hailed this shift from an exclusively internal scholasticate model to a university setting at the heart of Christendom. Among them were Pajot and Pinardy, proponents both of quality education for young Missionaries-to-be. They welcomed the opportunity to issue a call for higher standards at all levels, noting that "untrained educators and hasty improvisations could only prove costly, a truism that had been regrettably overlooked in the early days" [Jaouen, 1953: 120].

The members of the Chapter preparatory commission for classical studies, Eugène Beaup, Brissaud and Chanaron, recommended that the Apostolic Schools in Corps and Grenoble "adopt and implement a coherent program of courses." While the Hartford Apostolic School was still in its preliminary planning stages, Pajot was pleased to announce that Julien Ginet and Louis Sorrel were at that very moment in residence with the Sulpicians at St. Charles College in Ellicott City, Maryland, "to improve their English and acquaint themselves with the curriculum and principles of secondary education in the United States."

At the threshold of this expansionist era in the history of the Congregation, the Chapter awarded priority to its Apostolic Schools, an invaluable source of vocations and a security for the years ahead.

Next on the agenda were progress reports on recent foundations, and so the Capitulars delighted to hear that the parishes staffed by their colleagues in Danielson, Fitchburg and Hartford were thriving, materially and spiritually; that the irksome ethnic turmoil that had attended their coming to Danielson showed signs now of abating; that, faced with the challenge of accommodating 300 pupils in St. Joseph's three-classroom school, Vignon had decided to build a brand-new one; that a recent bazaar had netted $2,700.00, a magnificent contribution to the cause on the part of the struggling parishioners.

They learned, too, that the mission band was keeping a hectic schedule—and though tongue-twister place names such as the Connecticut towns of Bridgeport, New Haven, Wauregan, and Winsted meant little to them, knowing that Mary's message was reaching an expanding audience of responsive listeners had to mean a great deal to the Chapter Delegates; that retreats to women religious had, of late, opened welcome opportunities for preaching the spirit of La Salette; that in response to need and despite their as yet halting acquaintance with the language, the men had ventured into English-speaking parishes on weekend ministry; that their instructions to reply "all right" in answer to any and every question that might be put to them had given rise to several tight spots and a number of humorous episodes.

They were informed that a comfortable, functional and spacious college had in record time gone up on New Park Avenue, but that debt reduction was not likely to break any records; and told the great news that the Hartford Community—till now a group of Frenchmen, striving to adapt to the ways of the New World—was eagerly anticipating the entrance of the first class of U.S. students and "the real birth of the Congregation's American branch."

The Chapter then turned its attention to a series of reports on prospective foundations. The omnipresent threat of government interference notwithstanding, the men in France had been considering two new ministries: La Salette du Mont Saint-Clair, a shrine to Our Lady Reconciler at Sète, and an orphanage at Villeurbanne. Endorsed by the Capitulars, both proposals would be implemented within a year's time.

Sensing, quite accurately, that the full fury of the anticlerical storm was yet to be unleashed, the General Council urged the Chapter to look at several alternative refuges beyond France's borders for Apostolics and Novices. Belgium, Holland, Luxembourg, Switzerland, and Westphalia were mentioned as possible foundation sites.

Expansion plans would fall short of their mark, some argued, if the lack of a vital foreign mission thrust were not compensated. Despite the strain on the Congregation's sparse financial and personnel reserves, the reluctant withdrawal from Norway in 1892 had created a void that needed to be filled. The Chapter, therefore, enjoined the next General Administration to explore with the Congregation for the Propagation of the Faith the possible assignment of a mission field to each of the Institute's two sectors: France and the United States.

Given the Third Republic's history of arbitrary and discriminatory intrusions on their life and ministry, the religious in France, generally, disinclined to submit to civil authority. They had, for the most part, simply ignored the Accretion Tax Law of 1884. During the short-lived and permissive presidency of Pierre Casimir-Perier (1847-1907) the government had chosen to believe that the religious were failing to comply because the legislation itself—a variation for religious communities on France's inheritance tax laws—was excessively intricate.

Under Leftist pressure, Casimir-Perier had unexpectedly resigned and been succeeded in early 1895 by Felix Faure. Appointed Prime Minister by the new President, Alexandre Ribot (1842-1923) declared himself a partisan of Church-State appeasement, admonishing that he was not necessarily prepared to let

In March of 1895, French Prime Minister Alexandre Ribot (1842-1923) personally introduced a Subscription Tax Bill seen as unjust by many people

the Church have everything its own way. The Accretion Tax had generated 1,500,000 francs in 1890; revenues dropped to 350,000 francs in 1893 and had been plunging steadily since. In the Premier's view, the intricacy of the law was less at fault than the brilliant ingenuity with which the religious sidestepped its prescriptions.

In March of 1895, Ribot personally introduced a Subscription Tax Bill that called for a percentage of 0.30 francs to be levied annually on the capital value of all property owned by the religious. The measure speedily passed both the Chamber of Deputies and the Senate.

Most congregations and orders had countered this latest anticlerical financial offensive by adopting a passive resistance stance. The Chapter faced a distasteful dilemma. Should the Congregation, in solidarity with virtually all the religious and against the known wishes of Leo XIII, who made no secret of the fact that open hostility to the Republican regime was not to his liking, refuse to file the required declarations and forms with the Ministry of the Treasury?

All concurred that the law was "an unjust enactment and an iniquitous burden." Failure to comply, some cautioned, could well mean harsh penalties in the form of substantial fines. The passive resistance proposal carried, though not unanimously.

In mid-November the Chapter Delegates elected to a three-year term general officers whose work was cut out for them: Superior General, Joseph Perrin; Assistants General, Auguste Chapuy, Jean-Claude Villard, Celestin Thomas, and Pierre Pajot; Treasurer General, Auguste Ploussu.

Joseph Pinardy was appointed Director General of Studies, succeeding Jean-Claude Villard. Two new positions were created: Procurator to the Holy See (Auguste Blache, Superior of the Rome Scholasticate) and Vicar for the United States Region (Pierre Pajot, until such time as he assumed his duties as Councilor and Secretary General).

At the conclusion of the Chapter, the gathering singled out two stalwarts, conferring on them lifelong honorary membership on the General Council and consultative voice whenever present at its meetings. So honored were Pierre Archier and Jean Berthier. Their unstinting leadership and unwavering hope had greatly contributed over the years to the viability of the Institute.

Though he would remain a La Salette Missionary until his death in 1908, Berthier had—in response to a personal call—founded the Missionaries of the Holy Family and provided the expanding La Salette Congregation with an offshoot, a unique sign of growth.

Enamored of formation ministry from the day the Apostolic School opened at Corps in 1876, Berthier had long nurtured a vision all his own: the enlistment of belated vocations for service in the foreign missions. Having resigned as Director of the Loèche House of Studies in 1889, he returned to the mission band, his first love.

While conducting a retreat for the clergy of Rheims in 1893, he had the opportunity to share his dream with Benoît-Marie Langenieux (1824-1905), the Cardinal Archbishop, who was enthralled by what this La Salette retreat master had to say: "Two thirds of the globe dwells in the darkness of infidelity, heresy or schism. Three fourths of humanity have not heard of Our Lord. This world belongs to the merchants, who for the sake of material gain are willing to travel anywhere on earth, exploiting lands and peoples; Christians are hesitant to go forth for the sake of the Gospel. The harvest is plentiful, but the harvesters are few. Why not tap that reserve of recruits our seminaries turn away because of their age?"

Benoît-Marie Langenieux (1824-1905), Cardinal Archbishop of Rheims; watercolor by William Ewart Lockhart; photo: Bamfords Auctioneers & Valuers

The cherished project, through Langenieux's intermediary, was given papal blessing and endorsement in November of 1894. On January 11, 1895, the Generalate issued this laconic decision [Hostachy, 1946: 443]: "At his request, the General Council authorizes Reverend Father Jean Berthier to devote himself to a project promoting delayed vocations for service in the foreign missions, a project favored and fostered by the Sovereign Pontiff and His Eminence Cardinal Langenieux."

The house in Grave, Netherlands, where Fr. Jean Berthier, M.S., founded the Missionaries of the Holy Family

Along the way, communication appears to have broken down. Berthier's venture began to pose a threat to the General Council, as one must infer from Langenieux's letter of January 22, 1895, to Chapuy [Hostachy, 1946: 443]: "I understand your apprehensions concerning the project good Father Berthier is pursuing. But you are in a better position than he to eliminate their cause and, as a result, turn into blessings for your religious family what you see as a grave peril. Make it a point to tell everyone you meet how proud you are to see one of your sons, one who remains one with you in heart and, during the pilgrimage season, one who is with you in fact, charged with so great a mission for the Church."

Langenieux approved the Constitutions of the new Institute and invited Berthier to select a site for the first foundation. Berthier wisely chose not to settle in France. That September, a former military installation—barracks, hospital and parade grounds—in Grave, Holland, became the mother house of the Missionaries of the Holy Family.

Within months of his death on January 2, 1899, Archier willingly agreed to give a conference to the Apostolics in Grenoble. Then in his eighty-fourth year, the patriarch of the La Salette Missionaries, delivered this rather touching *Nunc Dimittis* [Hostachy, 1946: 415]:

"For more than thirty years, my children, we were no more than a dozen Brothers and Fathers. I dreamed all the while that the little Community might someday take wing for the sake of the good Mother's work, and I always had high hopes for our future. Never would I have dreamed, however, that I would live to see so much growth, and especially in such a short time. In less than twenty years we have gone from 10 to 150 professed religious. And still, throughout that interim, so many, having put their hand to the plow (Luke 9:62), lost heart. We should once again exclaim: 'For if this endeavor or this activity is of human origin, it will destroy itself.39But if it comes from God, you will not be able to destroy them...' (Acts 5:38-39), who would have destroyed it twenty times over, if they could have."

The future beckoned. Meeting its challenge would require gritty resolve. Fulfilling its promise would depend on the providential guidance of God and the sacrificial response of the men. In the first of his informative and popular circular letters, the new Superior General called attention to the Congregation's impressive statistics: Fathers 67, Scholastics 42, Brothers 14, Novices 12, Oblates 2, and Apostolics 75. He viewed the continued growth of the Institute as essentially contingent upon new opportunities to serve and the availability and readiness of personnel to take up these new ministries.

A Time for Planting

The time sadly came in May of 1898 for Pajot to leave the New World foundation that had been his pride and joy for six prodigious years and take up his General Administration duties in Grenoble. Socquet replaced him as superior in Hartford, Guinet replaced Socquet as pastor of St. James in Danielson, Vignon, now Vicar for the U.S. Region, replaced Guinet as pastor of Our Lady of Sorrows in Hartford, and Triquet replaced Vignon as pastor of St. Joseph's in Fitchburg.

Guinet brought his own brand of courtesy, friendliness and openness to the delicate situation in Danielson. Recognizing the need for a larger church, the new pastor was inspired to enlist the cooperation of the men. He invited them to clear the land and dig the foundation themselves. Grumblings were heard here and there, but the overall response was cheerful and enthusiastic. With proud heft and determination, the men of St. James got the job done. A troubled flock had come together in a united effort toward a common goal. Deep differences and sharp divisions, though not forgotten, were transcended.

La Salette College in Harford, CT opening its doors on Friday, Sept. 16, 1898; this is the class for that year

Perrin's Circular Letter #3, dated July 19, 1898, conveyed a baleful message. Wiser heads had not, in fact, prevailed at the Chapter the previous autumn. The worst fears voiced there by some had come true: "Having fined us for nonpayment of the taxes assessed by the Subscription Law that so iniquitously burdens our real estate, the Treasury is now seeking a court order to attach our residence in Noiretable. We obviously have no choice but to maintain the passive resistance posture our last Chapter imposed on us; we are nonetheless taking every precaution to shield ourselves from tracking by the Ministry of the Treasury."

In late August, the French-Canadians of Connecticut held their annual congress in Jewett City. Attempts, however strenuous and sustained, to oust the La Salettes from Danielson had foundered. Outdone, Leclaire conceded as much in his intervention at the gathering [Rumilly, 1965: 167]: "We are losing ground. The Bishop is partial to these French Communities that are scarcely preferable to Irish pastors. At this point, the La Salette Missionaries are entrenched in Danielson."

La Salette College in Hartford opened its doors on Friday. September 16, 1898. Louis Sorrel, "a man of strong constitution of agile and eager mind," its first Director, extended the warmest of welcomes to twelve American boys. Of the original class enrolled that day, three reached the goal of the La Salette Missionary priesthood: Zotique Chouinard (1883-1964), Emile Plante (1884-1954), and Armand Potvin (1883-1916).

To supply for in-house deficiencies, two laymen had been hired to teach English and mathematics. A cherished dream had come true. The American branch of the Institute was now a reality.

Two months later, word of Leo XIU's approval reached the General Council. Mission territories in Madagascar and Saskatchewan would become the responsibility of the La Salette Missionaries, subject to terms yet to be negotiated with the respective local ordinaries.

The year 1898 closed on a somber note: "The Treasury has instituted proceedings against the residence in Vienne," Perrin wrote in his Circular Letter #4 of December 18. "It would seem that, though heavily mortgaged, it is on the point of being confiscated. The bogus Subscription Law continues to mean substantial fines for unpaid taxes, even on a few parcels of land we had been obliged to buy when the road from St. Joseph's to the Shrine was being built."

Anxieties about the future of the Community and the fate of its holdings in France were set aside momentarily, as Constant Glatigny, Marius Michel, and Joseph Moussier were ordained to the priesthood in Hartford's St. Joseph Cathedral on September 8, 1899.

Accompanied by Vignon, now the Regional Vicar, Jules Morard set out from Hartford for the Canadian Northwest that fall. The men traveled by train from Hartford to Montreal. A forty-eight-hour train ride took them from Montreal to Winnipeg. Winnipeg to Areola, Saskatchewan, was another twelve hours. Having journeyed several days by horse and buggy, they at last reached Alma, the central mission post that had been agreed upon with Adélard Langevin (1855-1915), OMI, Archbishop of St. Boniface, Manitoba.

At Mass in the plank-hut church on Sunday, November 19, Morard read to the happy congregation the decree that established their parish and dedicated it to Our Lady of La Salette. Solitude would be no stranger to the missionary pastor on the virgin prairie, where buffalo herds roamed freely, summer sizzled, and winter brought raging blizzards and violent windstorms.

A Time for Uprooting

Paul-Emile Henry (1851-1911) was installed as Bishop of Grenoble on March 15, 1900

To curtail costly dunning by the Treasury, Perrin had transferred the titles to some of the Community's properties to the diocese. A subterfuge commonly resorted to by the religious, this practice was termed "interposition of persons" and declared illegal. Fava died on October 17, 1899. By law, the administration of all diocesan real estate and revenue was taken over, *sede vacante (the seat being vacant)*, by the State. Before the installation of Paul-Emile Henry (1851-1911) as Bishop of Grenoble on March 15, 1900, the French government had decreed the liquidation at public auction of 4,000,000 francs worth of diocesan property.

Eleven lots were put on the block, including the land and buildings at St. Joseph's in Corps and five acres of meadow on the south slope of Mount Planeau that the Institute owned. (The pastureland on the Holy Mountain was eventually repurchased; for want of a buyer, the property in Corps had not changed hands.) Perrin was less enchanted than ever with the idea of passive resistance!

A quick note he dispatched to Louis Beaup on March 20, 1900, affords the rare glimpse of a harried Joseph Perrin: "Am overworked. Am leaving right now for Lyons to keep an eye on our [Villeurbanne] residence there. The St. Joseph property is up for sale. Several Fathers in Vienne and Grenoble are unwell. Good news though from America and Madagascar, at least."

Written on Good Friday, April 13, 1900, Perrin's Circular Letter #8 presents a lucid interpretation of the times and calls persecution by its name. It includes an exhortation that draws deeply from the wellsprings of the La Salette Missionary's spirituality:

> "There can be no misreading the persecutory leanings of our ruling party. As we write these lines on the very day of the death of the Son of God made man for the salvation of the world, we feel the need to recall the words this divine Savior spoke to his apostles:"

It interprets the signs of the times in the light of Christ's own words and advances two certitudes: the inevitability of persecution and the assurance of victory:

> "'No slave is greater than his master.' If they persecuted me, they will also persecute you" (John 15:20).
>
> "Trust in me nevertheless ..." (John 14:2).
>
> "Go, therefore, make disciples of all the nations ..." (Matthew 28:19).
>
> "I have overcome the world ..." (John 16:33).
>
> "... and the gates of the netherworld will never prevail against (my church)" (Matthew 16:18).

On first reading, the third quotation could appear intrusive. In Perrin's sampler of Scripture verses, however, it plays the pivotal role. By placing it at the very heart of his interpretation, Perrin suggests that, since persecution is not coincidental to the spread of the Gospel, the appropriate response to it is not a pessimistic reaction but hope-filled evangelical action: "Go, therefore, and make disciples ..." (Matthew 28:19). Not surprisingly, he goes on to cite the traditional La Salette Parallel between the risen Christ's apostolic commission and Our Lady's maternal commission to Melanie and Maximin:

> "And this is also what our merciful Mother told us twice at the end of her Apparition: *Well, my children, you will make this known to all my people.*"

In this painting entitled "Our Lady of La Salette, Reconciler of Sinners" by M. Barberis, Mary invites her people to "make this message known to all (her) people."

Refraction, one might say, served to describe the basic La Salette dynamic. The Apparition refracted the light rays and energy waves of the Gospel through the prism of its message, symbolism and tears. This word of liberating truth illuminated an entire spectrum of specific evils. In its pained yet compassionate accents, the La Salette utterance faithfully echoed the lament of Jesus for Jerusalem: "If this day you only knew what makes for peace—but now it is hidden from your eyes... " (Luke 19:42).

Prophecy extends this same divine pity to every generation [St. Thomas Aquinas, *Summa Theologica*, 2a-2ae, q. 174, a. 6]: "In every age there has not been lacking the spirit of prophecy, not indeed for the revelation of new doctrines of faith, but for the guidance of human action, because as it is written: 'Without a vision the people lose restraint; but happy is the one who follows instruction'" (Proverbs 29:18).

"Yes, Reverend Fathers, let us go on making known to the Christian people the saving news of the Gospel and the teachings of the heavenly Apparition; doing so not only by our preaching and the dedicated ingenuity an unflinching and enlightened zeal might inspire, but especially by the no less eloquent and so readily understood preaching of the good example we give and the spiritual lives we are living, never allowing ourselves to be thwarted either by the wickedness of the world, or by opposition of any kind, or even by our own failings."

Just as it had twenty years before, when the first government decrees threatened France's religious with expulsion, the watchword resounded loud and clear: "... proclaim the word; be persistent whether it is convenient or inconvenient; convince, reprimand, encourage through all patience and teaching" (2 Timothy 4:2). Proclaiming the word in a compelling, moving, and relevant way was more necessary than ever. Resting on solid theological ground, this response also verified a fundamental sociological principle: The ideology with which a group has negotiated a major transition or overcome a major hurdle is likely to remain its doctrine thereafter.

A severe test would come in July of the next year with the passing of the Associations Law. Press coverage of its progress through the legislative process convinced Perin that enactment of this measure banning religious communities outright was only a matter of time. His canonical visit to the United States and Canada would, however, bring needed respite from pressing cares and a welcome opportunity to breathe the air of American freedom.

A man of action and adventure, Perrin was fascinated—as he recounted later in some detail—at the sight of a thirty-story skyscraper in New York; a priest and religious superior, he was impressed by the attendance at Sunday Mass in Danielson, Fitchburg and Hartford and awed by the sizable parochial school enrollment. A letter he sent to the General Councilors on May 25 captures his enthusiasm and excitement:

> "I set foot on American soil one week ago today and have been living almost like an American. I thought the ocean voyage was just about ideal. When seasickness overtook them,

our three Scholastics [Victor Faure (1881-1959), Eugène Veillard (1883-1960) and Albert Rosset (1883-1967)] formed a different impression. Father Vignon was at the pier to meet us when we arrived on Saturday, May 19. Clearing our baggage through customs took a while, and as a result we did not get to Hartford until 3:00 am. ... Everywhere in the city, there is feverish industrial activity. The railroad has five parallel tracks and a rapid train system that radiates in all directions. The American people, in my opinion, are serious-minded, hardworking and practical in their comfortable way of life."

Beaming with pride, the Superior General joined with the Danielson Community on Pentecost, June 3, as the cornerstone of the new St. James' Church was blessed by Tierney. A crowd of 3,000 attended the ceremony. Two sermons were delivered, one in English and one in French.

A Time for Scattering

Michael Tierney (1839-1908) became the sixth Bishop of Hartford on February 22, 1894

Circular Letter #10 of January 19, 1901, records Perrin's somber reflections on the impending passage of the Associations Law. An ominous premonition raised the question: "Shall we be required to drink the bitter cup of the good Mother's tears?"

> "These are trying times. We repeat: dies mali sunt (Ephesians 5:16). Our Community's survival is at stake. Now is the time to multiply our supplications and virtuous deeds. Now is the time to act. I earnestly entreat your charitable prayers. Raise your arms to heaven and storm its portals with a holy violence. What is now at stake is not simply whether or not our Fathers will be allowed to go on ministering but the triumph of God's cause and that of God's Church. At stake is the preservation of all our religious Congregations in France. Hell is bent on destroying them by any possible means. By the tears

of Our Lady of La Salette, we implore you: critical ills call for drastic remedies."

Given the Congregation's strong ties to the Shrine at La Salette, the General Council at one point did consider the advisability of seeking legal authorization. To that end, the makings of a dossier had been compiled. A blunt and peremptory statement by the Bishop of Grenoble, however, quashed the move. In the course of a discussion Perrin and Pinardy were having with him at the episcopal residence, Bishop Henry said to the Superior General [Hostachy, 1946: 418]: "'In your case, Father, authorization is out of the question. Should you submit the request, it will be denied.' The new Bishop proved to be no less cutting than the icy sword wielded by the State."

Strenuously resisted by the congregations and sporadically enforced by the government, the Accretion Tax and the Subscription Tax Laws undeniably failed to attain their objective. In October of 1899, Waldeck-Rousseau, the Premier, had introduced a measure designed to deal France's refractory religious the ultimate blow. Reviving the distinction between authorized and unauthorized orders, the proposed Associations Bill stipulated that all congregations were to request authorization or be expelled from the country. It was no secret, however, that the National Assembly intended to grant legal authorization in the rarest of cases.

The Law of Associations was passed on July 1, 1901.

In late July, the sad news was communicated to the Congregation: "After prayer and consultation, the General Council has decided not to seek legal authorization. Those Fathers who remain in France will be secularized. The others, together with the Scholastics and Apostolics, will go either to Tournai, Belgium, or to Massongex, Switzerland. The Novices will go to Salmata, Italy."

Six priests stayed on in France, two of whom—Casimir Gachet and Jean Angelier (1870-1939)—resided at l'Hermitage. This half-dozen men continued to conduct parish missions as secular priests. A small remnant, they were especially pleased to exercise the charism of the Institute in their homeland at a time when it most needed to hear

Our Lady's message.

On September 20, the Ministry of Justice sent an official notice to public prosecutors all over France, reminding them that the period for requesting authorization would expire on October 3. Unauthorized congregations that had neither dispersed nor requested authorization, the circular specified, would be immediately subjected to liquidation procedures.

Between September 21 and 27, Louis Comte (1860-1934), Eugène Beaup (1866-1929) and Fernand Patarin (1862-1939), together with some twenty Aposolics, fled in three small bands from Grenoble to Tournai. "Moving, bag and baggage, between the Gare de Lyon and the Gare du Nord they offered people strolling in the streets of Paris a spectacle to behold. A trotting cortege of hackneys. The first, overflowing with bundled bedding, featured a priest, crucifix dangling loose at the waist, bracing himself against the driver, stretching his arm to steady an intractable load. The other two displayed smalltown boys in their Sunday best, hair dishevelled, eyes reddened by lack of sleep or weeping, peering out from a helter-skelter of trunks and suitcases" [Jaouen, 1953: 116].

A frequent pilgrim to the Holy Mountain, the kindly pastor of Sacred Heart in Tournai extended to these expatriates the temporary hospitality of his parish youth center. Flimsy partitions and a vivid imagination transformed the spacious, though dank and drafty, hall into a seminary: dormitory, refectory and study area. Castoff chairs, sawhorse tables, two dozen or so dressers, each of them bearing an uncanny resemblance to a steamer trunk, and stacks of hastily unpacked books signaled the end of an interlude and the start of serious business. A gypsy camp atmosphere nonetheless prevailed. These makeshift premises had to be vacated regularly—partitions dismantled, and personal belongings stowed away—in deference to the parish's weekly card party.

With heartfelt thanksgiving, the Tournai Community moved into a place of its own twenty months later, a memorable April 29, 1903.

Soon after October 3, the local judiciary proceeded against all unauthorized establishments that had not filed a request. Municipal authorities dispatched a justice of the peace to determine whether the religious not seeking authorization had dispersed. If they had gone, the local court named a liquidator to dispose of the property. If it was discovered that an unauthorized order had neither requested authorization nor abandoned its house, it was held to be in violation of the Law of Associations. An injunction was then sought, and a court-appointed liquidator eventually disposed of the property.

All requests for authorization, the Council of State had ruled, were to be submitted to the National Assembly as proposals that either house, acting independently, could definitively accept or reject. This allowed the government to put before the Senate the half-dozen cases it was willing to let through, condemning the rest to abolition in the Chamber of Deputies.

The majority in the anticlerical Chamber did plummet to a mere sixteen votes, however, when eighty-one congregations of women were dissolved in a single package-vote. Honor among thieves. Shame among anti-clericals.

The Residence on Rue Chanrion in Grenoble yielded the State 64,000 francs at auction. The St. Joseph property in Corps went into the liquidator's hands. Casimir Gachet and Jean Angelier served a twenty-five-day jail sentence for staying on at l'Hermitage beyond the October 3 deadline. Perrin and his Assistants moved to Massongex in the Swiss canton of Valais, where they established the La Salette Generalate-in-Exile.

Massongex in the Swiss canton of Valais is where the La Salette Generalate-in-Exile was established

Four eventful years at the head of the Institute had elapsed. "Those abominable laws and their devastating aftermath" sorely grieved Perrin, but the callousness of the Bishop of Grenoble pained him almost as deeply.

On his return from Henry's consecration in early 1900, Perrin had shared with an intimate his first impression of the new Ordinary: "A good child, but a child!" A priest of the Diocese of Montpellier, Paul-Emile Henry was "a bright man, a doctor in theology, a renowned preacher, and an acclaimed lecturer at the University of Montpellier. He served with distinction in a variety of pastoral ministries, including the pastorate of the largest parish in the see city. His episcopal aspirations, he expended little effort to conceal. His markedly Republican leanings, well-known at the Ministry of Cults, anything but hindered his promotion to Grenoble. A timid, unsure soul, he was dependent on the counsel of a select few and was easily influenced, swayed and, at times, duped" [Bligny, 1979: 236].

The relationship between the Congregation and Fava's successor were strained from the outset. One of the vicars general and an attorney for the diocese would have turned the newly-installed Bishop against the La Salette Missionaries, suggesting that they had subtly manipulated his predecessor, were competing with the secular clergy for donations and popularity, were taking unfair fiscal advantage of their presence on the Holy Mountain, and generating financial support for their worldwide apostolates through the *Annales*, a publication linked in everyone's mind with the famous diocesan Shrine, and recommending that he be wary.

In a letter he sent to a friend in December of 1901, Perrin confided: "As far as Bishop Henry is concerned the Missionaries of Our Lady of La Salette are annihilated. It was inevitable that the pack surrounding this poor Pilate should someday cry out against us: *"tolle, tolle, crucifige [away with them, away with them, crucify them]!"*

As it sank in, the thought that Our Lady's Missionaries no longer ministered on her mountain haunted Perrin. He had spent thirty-seven years of his life at the Shrine. He and his esteemed colleague Jean Berthier had made their novitiate under the eminent La Salette spiritual master, Sylvain-Marie Giraud, and taken first vows up there on September 8, 1865, He in turn had served as Master of Novices at La Salette, forming Pierre Pajot and Louis Sorrel among others, to the religious life. For as long as anybody could remember he had discharged the duties of rector, superior, treasurer, and general overseer on that hallowed site.

Perrin blanched. Dismay followed upon disbelief. By decree of August 19, 1902, the Federal Council in Bern had moved to expel unwelcome religious from Swiss soil: "The establishment in Switzerland of Congregations and Orders whose names appear on the following list is forbidden in this country according to Article 52 of the Constitution. ..." The Missionaries of La Salette appeared on the roster of those banished—between the Carthusians and the Poor Clares, the very finest company under any other circumstances. The La Salette Generalate-in-Exile was provisionally transferred to Perugia, Italy.

A Time for Dying

Sent out from Italy on August 19, 1903, Circular Letter #11 offered a retrospective on the convulsive events of the recent past. Reeling still from the multiple blows anticlericalism had dealt the Institute, the Superior General viewed this tragic period in its history as a time of divine pruning and purification:

Joseph Perrin, M.S. (1897-1913) was the fourth La Salette Superior General

> "Great and terrible ordeals have befallen our dear religious family since we drafted our last circular on January 19, 1901! Our expulsion from the Holy Mountain, the disbanding and dispersion of our community in France, the loss of our properties, exile, our flight to Switzerland, and then to Italy, all of these trials visited upon us by divine Providence will remain engraved forever as sad moments in our

Congregation's history."

Freighted with moral outrage and resentment, Perrin's words become defiant at one point:

> "Before the gates of hell we will retreat only one step at a time, and even then, only most grudgingly."

A postmortem in question and answer form brings his comments to a close:

> "What more could we have done in the face of those anti-religious laws, laws that our H. Father Leo XIII, of blessed memory, characterized as iniquitous and contrary to the natural law?"

> "We could do no more than pray, consult, and act in accordance with our own best interests. This is exactly what we did when we opted to be officially dissolved m France rather than consent to a humiliating and futile compliance."

When the General Council opted in 1901 "to be officially dissolved in France," the La Salette Missionaries had been present and at work in the New World for nearly ten years. Travail, as might have been expected, accompanied this birth-giving. The seeming accidents of history had supplied birth pangs. The spreading Institute experienced firsthand the hard truth of what the Hebrew sage had so matter-of-factly recited: "There is an appointed time for everything, and a time for every affair under the heavens. A time to give birth, and a time to die; a time to plant, and a time to uproot the plant" (Ecclesiastes 3:1-2). The "grain of wheat" motif (John 12:24) had put its authenticating seal on the Congregation's longed-for expansion.

The guarantee of religious liberty presented a decided advantage and a welcome opportunity for unhampered development. This, none would deny. Some believed, however, that the cult of comfort, convenience and materialism, which had become synonymous in many a European mind with the American way of life, might threaten the ascetical and sacrificial dimensions of the La Salette vocation. They stood instinctively with those members of the United States hierarchy who were less than optimistic about the outcome of the Church's head-on encounter with the spirit of the modern world on American soil.

At this juncture, a renewed effort was made to secure a spiritual center strong enough to withstand the detected and undetected centrifugal forces operative in the massive displacement. The forcible expulsion from the Holy Mountain added weight to the concern. "More than a symbol of its unity, this shrine had been the scene of the Institute's continual creation in heart-to-heart talks with the Mother of Sorrows" [Jaouen, 1953: 132]. Hence the need to consider the Rule as a unifying charter, articulating a shared vision and common mission, to be observed by the worldwide brotherhood.

This objective was uppermost in mind as the General Chapter met in Villarfocchiardo, Italy, on July 2 through 28, 1903.

In response to the *Norms for Institutes of Simple Vows* issued by the Congregation of Bishops and Regulars in 1901, the Delegates tussled once more with a revision project. Among the conclusions and decisions they reached, the following appear to be particularly noteworthy: the whole Congregation (rather than the Chapter or the General Council) was said to be seeking the favor of papal approbation for its Constitutions; the widespread dispersion of its members was cited as an additional and compelling reason for granting this approval: "that, given their dispersal to all parts of the globe in these most recent times, all its members may by closer ties be bound to one another and to the Institute itself."

To expedite the Curia's task of reviewing and approving such documents at a time when applications for pontifical approval were proliferating, the Norms prescribed a standardized, uniform format for drafting Constitutions. Only those constitutive canonical elements that were binding on all religious could henceforth be included. Distinctive elements, such as the scriptural, spiritual and inspirational texts proper to each Institute, were relegated to the general directory.

Stripped of their explicit La Salette referent, the *Constitutions* of 1903 nevertheless preserve a sharp traditional focus: **mission**— " ... to combat contemporary crimes" [no. 4] (in deference to the times, the classical ills and evils were upgraded to crimes); *spirit*—"... of prayer, penance and zeal" [no. 5]; *wellspring*— "Its members draw this spirit from their meditation on the sufferings of Our Lord and the sorrows of the Blessed Virgin Mary" [no. 6].

The work mostly of Louis Beaup, novice master for forty years, the General Customary of 1903 provided the essential La Salette component then struck from the *Constitutions*. While fleshing out the generic reference to meditation on "the sorrows of the Blessed Virgin Mary" [no. 6], for example, it effects a radical shift of locus from the historic site of the inaugural Vision to the heart of the La Salette Missionary—wherever he might be called to minister—as he contemplates the three phases of the Apparition and reflects on their pastoral implications.

"Torn from their cradle, exiled from their Mother House, the Fathers would have to carry more vividly than ever the seeds of the 'founding event' in their hearts and make Mary's message echo from the mountain heights of their own zealous dedication" [Barrette, 1975: 30].

The fundamental La Salette Equation remained operative. Reduced to its simplest terms, this basic identification—harking back to Denaz's insight in the 1850s—meant that had there been no Apparition at La Salette, there would be no La Salette Missionaries. The Institute's "continual creation" must ever spring uninterruptedly from intimate conversations with Our Lady.

An address delivered by a Scholastic on August 5, 1901. the twenty-fifth anniversary of the founding of the Apostolic School in Corps, offers a rare rank-and-file statement of the La Salette identity and a glimpse of missionary militancy at the height of the crisis-expansion period [Missionnaires de La Salette, [1902: 75-76]:

> "Italy is telling us: I am Mary's people. France is telling us: I am Mary's people. Switzerland is telling us: I am Mary's people. Scandinavia is telling us: I am Mary's people. Africa in turn exclaims: I am Mary's people. The immense American continent joins in: I am Mary's people.

"In a word, all nations are claiming their share in Calvary's bequest: 'Behold, your mother' (John 19:27).

"We are her accredited ambassadors to all nations. And what she asks of us is that we should work to eradicate the major crimes of our day, which she herself came among us to bewail. Now, it is not only in the land of La Salette that Sunday rest is violated, that the laws of fast and abstinence are trampled underfoot, that the holy name of God is blasphemed. "Behold, all the nations are wicked and vain are their works" (Isaiah 59:6 [Vulgate]). Adapting it to ourselves, we take St. Cyprian's saying as our motto: *The La Salette Missionary may be put to death, but he never surrenders (Missionarius Salettensis occidi potest, vinci non potest)*. Forward, then! With the Gospel in one hand and the Virgin's Discourse in the other we shall march off tomorrow to conquer in the footsteps of our glorious predecessors. Meanwhile, the United States, Canada, and Madagascar are calling upon her 'who wishes to be honored and invoked throughout the universe' (Litany of Our Lady of La Salette)."

Detail from "Christ on the Cross with Mary and St. John" (c. 1457-1460) by Rogier van der Weyden (1399-1464); photo by WikiArt.org

A Time for Giving Birth

After an absence of four years, Pajot returned to the United States in 1902 as canonical visitor. A decade before, he and Vignon—their hopes alternately soaring and sagging—had gone from chancery to chancery in search of a firm offer. A decade later, the roles were reversed. Ironically enough, the bishops were submitting the requests. In a letter he wrote to Perrin on April 24, 1902, for instance, Bishop Paul Larocque of Sherbrooke, Quebec, offered the parish in Stanstead, outlining its appealing features: "Besides the regular income from the parish the Fathers could preach missions in Sherbrooke and in neighboring dioceses as well, all of which would provide the community with ample funds for all its needs. ... A truly apostolic undertaking which would strengthen the faith of the Catholics in that area, bring about the probable conversion of many Protestants, ... most of the population, and considering the number of friends you would make among the laity not only in the diocese but among Canadian Catholics everywhere, much good would accrue to your own Congregation."

At the invitation of John Farley, Archbishop of New York, the Community took on the care of St. Francis de Sales Parish in Phoenicia; Vignon became its first La Salette pastor on April 20, 1902. He had happily served in the Catskills only a few months when, to his keen disappointment, General Administration duties summoned him back to Europe.

During Perrin's canonical visit to the United States in 1900, Thomas Beaven (1851-1920), the Bishop of Springfield, had enlisted the Superior General's assistance in meeting a pastoral challenge. For want of priests conversant in their native tongue, the spiritual needs of the growing population of Polish immigrants in his diocese were going largely unmet. Perrin pledged the Congregation's help.

To prepare for this specialized ministry in the western part of Massachusetts, five Swiss La Salette Missionaries, recently ordained in Rome—Joseph Fux (1872-1913), Oswald Loretan (1876-1964), Salomon Schalbetter (1873-1934), Francis Schnyder (1872-1929) and Gabriel

from left: Some La Salettes who went to serve in Poland: Oswald Loretan (1876-1964), Francis Schnyder (1872-1929) and Gabriel Van Roth (1875-1941)

Van Roth (1875-1941)—were sent to Poland to familiarize themselves with its faith heritage and religious customs, all the while mastering its language. They reached Krakow on September 16, 1902, and took up residence there with the Vincentians, their attentive hosts and patient tutors for two years.

Two months into their total immersion program, the rudiments of the language remained elusive [Missionnaires de La Salette, 1903: 22]: "We are all in good health, but our Polish is coming along rather slowly. In fact, we are yet to understand a thing that is being read in the refectory. This is none too encouraging." Fux and Loretan arrived in Hartford on December 20, 1904. On December 22, they met with Beaven, and one week later, their newly and arduously acquired proficiency met its true test as they took charge of St. Mary's Parish in Ware, Massachusetts.

On October 5, 1902, Etienne Cruveiller assumed the pastorate of Sacred Heart in Stanstead, Quebec, a few miles across the border from Derby Line, Vermont. Not long after they had settled in, the Missionaries of La Salette arranged to purchase a large city block behind the church with the intention of building a seminary like the one in Hartford at some future date.

A native son of Les Ablandins, and thus a man with deep twofold ties to La Salette, Clement Moussier set out from Hartford in the late autumn of 1902 for South America. He reached Santos, Brazil, on December 18 and began serving as chaplain to the Sisters of St. Joseph of Chambery and to the patients in the leprosarium they maintained there. Two years later, he was made pastor of St. Anne Parish in Saõ Paolo, where he also opened a La Salette residence, the mustard-seed sowing of the Province of the Immaculate Conception. The movement from France to the United States had now given rise to a movement from the United States, an early branching out. Hale and hearty, the offshoot had become a main stem.

One decade after their coming to America the Missionaries of Our Lady of La Salette had shaped a pattern of apostolic works that replicated the pattern established in France over the years: education-formation, parish missions, retreats to religious, foreign missions, centers and publications promoting the devotion to the Virgin Reconciler. The glaring difference—and a notable addition—being the administration and pastoral care of parishes.

In 1852, de Bruillard had appointed one of the three founding members of the diocesan missionary band parish priest at La Salette. Within months Denaz had, for the sake of community life and prayer, left the village rectory and joined his confreres on the mountain.

St. Ann's Church, our La Salette Parish and Shrine in Sao Paulo, Brazil

There can be little doubt that staffing a parish was an important part of the La Salette proposal Pajot and Vignon presented to bishop after bishop in the summer of 1892. Two years later, when Bishop Beaven of Springfield, made a firm offer of St. Joseph's Parish in Fitchburg, the General Chapter was in session.

Based on the United States' mission status, the accelerating increase in the number of parishes, the shortage of clergy fluent in the languages of immigrant Catholics, the perfect forum for instilling the message of reconciliation and steady source of income parishes would provide, the Regional Council built a strong case for including parish ministry among the apostolates engaged in by the Congregation. The Chapter voted its approval, amending the Constitutions to this effect and adding the proviso: "insofar as it might be necessary to achieve the apostolic end of the Institute" (Rule of 1894, 1, 1, no. 9), intimating that somehow a concession or exception was being made.

A full-length article in the December 1902 issue of the *Bulletin*, "La Salette in America: An Overview of the Devotion to Our Lady of La Salette," reported in glowing terms on the success of the gambit [Missionnaires de La Salette, 1902: 345-347]:

> "La Salette was known in the New World before the arrival of the Missionaries, but unfortunately by means of periodicals and books that brought its authenticity into doubt. It is not uncommon, particularly in Canada, to meet the finest people and, at times, even holy religious, who are convinced that La Salette has disappeared, annihilated by the blows of its detractors. In less than ten years the Fathers have opened six residences in North America; naturally, each of these centers is making the Queen of the Alps known and loved. In Hartford they staff an Irish parish and operate an apostolic school with a student body of forty boys. For all practical purposes, Hartford serves as the seat of American devotion to Our Lady. This past September the three traditional statuary groups were placed in a side chapel of Our Lady of Sorrows Church in order to portray the entire scene of the Apparition as accurately as possible. A painted panorama, reproducing the mountains at La Salette rather faithfully, provided an appropriate background."

Considerations of human prudence might have suggested that undertaking the mission in faraway Saskatchewan be deferred until the American foundation itself rested on more settled ground and more trained personnel had become available. The universality of the La Salette message, the parallel reading of Christ's command to the apostles and of Mary's parting words to the young cowherds, however, made a La Salette presence in that untamed vastness imperative. Morard labored there alone for better than a year against enormously challenging odds, as Perrin recognized in his Circular Letter #9, written on October 6, 1900, on his return from the first canonical visitation to Canada and the United States:

> "We wish to pay a special tribute of praise and admiration to Father Jules Morard, missionary pastor of Alma. The Ordinary, Archbishop Langevin himself, told me it required a man of genuine heroism to establish a parish in so remote and difficult a district. Like the Good Shepherd of souls, he has been devoting himself to the spiritual and temporal care of his flock, dispersed as it is over an area some one hundred miles in length."

Fr. Jules Morard, M.S. (1867-1954), Missionary Pastor in Alma, Saskatuan, Canada

An invaluable response to the needs of the fast-growing dioceses of the United States and Canada, a fulfilling outlet for the men's priestly zeal, an appreciated taproot of contributions and revenue, the La Salette parishes also functioned as hubs of missionary outreach and as centers, or mini-shrines, for spreading the devotion to Mary as Reconciler of sinners.

Preaching held pride of place among them. It served as a unifying thread that ran through much of what Our Lady's Missionaries were doing. While their sermons called for a personal imprint and allowed for an individual touch, preaching was not an entirely individualistic enterprise. The mission band repertory listed forty set topics to be treated in a prescribed sequence. The Constitutions stipulated that each of the regions should draw up its own customary for missions and retreats, "recalling to the Missionaries the traditions and customs of the Congregation adapted to local circumstances."

The General Customary for Missions described in some detail the style in which the instructions were to be delivered. Designed to offset common abuses, these directives could appear to have been lifted from any of the manuals in vogue at the time. On closer inspection, however, they disclose a methodology faithfully patterned on Mary's approach in her Apparition.

"In their sermons, the Missionaries aim at being simple and forceful." No barrier or distance in the form of oratorical posturing was to come between the speaker and his audience: "They carefully avoid studied elegance, affectation, long sentences." The message should be forceful—cogent and relevant "... devoid of triviality and cliché." An abuse of the power the ministry of the word confers, anger was not to be taken for forcefulness: "They avoid any display of indignation, spite, or impatience."

Concrete language, so characteristic of prophetic discourse, was also insistently urged: "They avoid expressions that are abstract or too technical." The preached word was oftentimes reinforced using graphics: standing against a backdrop of alpine peaks, the various phases of the Apparition evoked the well-defined contours of Mary's 1846 intervention. This approach verified the essential description of the prophetic charism: the concrete will of God spoken by God's living messenger into a concrete space-time situation.

Adjusting to the active, busy pace of life in America demanded little effort on the part of the pioneers. There had always been much to do in France, and few hands available to do it. A downright practical, spontaneous approach to things may have required some learning, but these men were determined to do things in America the American way [Duggan, 1930: 175]:

> "The Fathers of La Salette are apparently committed to a program of intensive progress. They are alive to the opportu-

nities which this country affords. In the interest of their community, they publish a monthly magazine which has about it, together with its inevitable flavor of asceticism, a tinge of advanced Americanism not to be expected in a paper taking its original inspiration from a Continental stronghold as conservative as Grenoble, France. If they undertake to run a farm it must be according to the most progressive methods. When a community of French brothers 'out-American' the American farmer, there need be no special apprehension respecting the ability of their superiors to imbibe what is best and sanest in the social and political life of the country."

Maurice McAuliffe (1875-1944), the eighth Bishop of Hartford, Connecticut

The Fathers and Brothers who settled in Hartford early on — although they seldom, if ever, said so in so many words— considered themselves not as immigrants among immigrants but as Missionaries to America, Our Lady's Missionaries to America. They willingly took on its customs, language and ways for the sole purpose of adapting her urgent plea and the witness of their vowed lives to the New World setting. They instinctively espoused the principle of missionary "assimilationism" advocated by the Apostle Paul: "I have become all things to all (people)" (1 Corinthians 9:22b).

They wholeheartedly embraced the melting-pot proposition; their mission transcended all national boundaries and ethnic rivalries. Where the implantation of the Institute in the United States, the nurture of the American branch of the Congregation was concerned, their own roots, heritage, and identity as Frenchmen receded.

In the prepared remarks he offered at the end of the Fiftieth Anniversary Mass celebrated in the Chapel of La Salette College on July 9, 1942, Maurice McAuliffe (1875-1944), the eighth Bishop of Hartford, paid insightful tribute to these courageous La Salette Founders in terms they themselves would have found intelligible [La Salette Missionaries, September 1942: 169]:

> "These heroic men came into this country, not as strangers and foreigners—they were one with the unbroken line of valiant European missionaries who blazed a trail for the spread of the Gospel in this land and built the early Church in America long before this country had won independent status."

For Your Reflection

Scripture: 2 Timothy 4:6-8 (Reward for fidelity)

"For I am already being poured out like a libation, and the time of my departure is at hand. I have competed well; I have finished the race; I have kept the faith. From now on the crown of righteousness awaits me, which the Lord, the just judge, will award to me on that day, and not only to me, but to all who have longed for his appearance."

Questions for reflection:

The La Salette Apparition has been described by biblical scholars as "the most biblical apparition." That may be why the La Salette Sisters, Brothers and Fathers as well as those laity who have traveled close with and often ministered beside La Salettes can identify with the scripture when it says, "These are trying times" (Ephesians 5:16). Perhaps they have also endured many challenges but can rest well at the end of their life and say with St. Paul, "For I am already being poured out like a libation, and the time of my departure is at hand. I have competed well; I have finished the race; I have kept the faith" (2 Timothy 4:7).

- What is a cross that you have borne for the love of God?

- Whom do you know who could have said with St. Paul at the end of their life: "I have competed well; I have finished the race; I have kept the faith"?

Prayer:

Mary, Mother of God's People, your journey with your own La Salette Community has been a long and challenging one. As laity and religious who are deeply rooted in the La Salette message and mission, we wish to praise God for giving you to us as a Reconciler of Sinners.

Your lasting words and example borne of our experience of your Apparition at La Salette are profound gifts from God for which are truly thankful. May we continue to make your message known to all your people, inspired by the persistence and dedication of the La Salette Missionaries – past and present.

We ask this through your loving intercession and through the grace of your Son who lives with the Father, and the Holy Spirit, one God, for ever and ever. Amen.

La Salette Invocation:

Our Lady of La Salette, Reconciler of Sinners, pray without ceasing for us who have recourse to you.

Chapter Seven:
The Past and The Future of Our Present

The Past of Our Present

Ralph Waldo Emerson (1803-1882), an American essayist, lecturer, philosopher, and poet

These reflections on our history at the turn of the century leave much unsaid; they leave many a fascinating tale untold. If there is any truth to Ralph Waldo Emerson's contention that "there is properly no history, but only biography," a detailed retelling and mindful reading of the story of each of our La Salette founders on American soil would be amply rewarded. In the restricted compass of this chronicle, their accomplishments stand barely sketched; their religious lives and lasting apostolic contributions to our history remain a pallid evocation.

As time-bound beings, ours is a three-dimensional awareness, encompassing past, present and future. Consciously or unconsciously, we always associate recollections of our past with hopes and fears for the future of our present.

We have not yet reached—please God—the end of our history but are struggling through it still. We trust the lessons of our impressive past might serve to point our troubled present towards the promise oi" its future. If it had indeed run its course, the full sweep of our history could he narrated from start to finish; and we would, of course, be able to assess the significance of each part for the whole. As it is, we must puzzle over the pieces of our past and tease out their fragmentary meaning.

"The past is never dead. It is not even past," a character in William Faulkner's *Intruders in the Dust* baldly declares. Our past, then, is with us yet. Is ours a usable past? What can it teach us? How has it conditioned our present? What might it augur for our future? If we would find answers to these questions, we must first claim and identity with our *past*, a past and as *our* past. Encountering and understanding the past on its own terms is no easy enterprise.

We do not so much live in a place and time as we do in a perception of a place and time. Our image of the world we live-in. of the Congregation in whose ranks we serve the world is only apparently impartial and objective. Subjectivity colors any assessment we make of the most empirical facts of our recent experience. This is truer still of our assessment of the past.

History sets out its store of more-or-less neutral and verifiable data under the Who? What? When? and Where? rubric: dates, decisions, events, names, places, movements and trends. written records and statements. The slide into the subjective occurs early on. however, as the historian reckons with the Why? Past assumptions, certitudes, mindsets, motivations and value systems prove more elusive by far.

If only we could go back to 1902. let us say, and eavesdrop on a parish mission instruction in Wauregan, a Sunday sermon in Fitchburg. a class at La Salette College in Hartford, an animated meeting of the Regional Council. Better still, how exhilarating and informative it would be to sit and exchange fraternal views on La Salette, reconciliation, contemporary events, our shared heritage and aspirations with any of the intensely committed men whose dormant memory these recollections might have reawakened!

Yet, there is a continuity between our present and our past. Our past and present are closely linked. These linkages come down to us in different guises: institutional continuities, persisting attitudes, traditional beliefs, inherited strengths and weaknesses, "genetic" characteristics and traits (dominant and recessive), and the enduring consequences of earlier decisions (actions and omissions).

Discontinuity is also a reality because change, paradoxically, is a constant. Inescapably, change attends all development and growth, all passage through time. We remain more aware of discontinuity than of continuity between the present and the past, though, for the simple reason that we know more—and in a livelier and more compelling way—about our own time and world than we do, or can, about a former time and world.

This imbalance inevitably skews our attempt to embrace the linkages between past and present. It overdetermines our effort in the direction of contemporary concerns, consciousness and presuppositions as we decide what is and what is not relevant to the inquiry. It was essential to our purpose, therefore, that several voices from the past be heard at some length in order to establish as authentic and broad a context as possible for the views they express.

While the General Chapter of May 1891 was exploring the possibilities and calculating the risks of a New World foundation, Leo XIII issued the celebrated Encyclical, *Rerum Novarum*, that ushered in the era of the Church in the modern world. The times, as the Pope surveyed them with consternation, were marked by the spirit of revolution, the overturning of thrones and the toppling of economic and political structures. They presaged a crisis in the spiritual order. No longer holding sway, former certainties, regimes and values had been cast off. There could be no turning back. It remained for the believer to infuse these "new things" with the perennial truths of faith and illumine these new realities with Gospel light.

In the encyclical he published on May 1, 1991, in commemoration of the one hundredth anniversary of *Rerum Novarum*, John Paul II invites us "to look back [at the 'new things' his predecessor addressed and against which our

John Paul II (1980)

forebears strived], to look around at the 'new things' which surround us and in which we find ourselves caught up, ... and to look to the future at a time when we can already glimpse the third millennium of the Christian era, so filled with uncertainties but also with promises" [*Centesimus Annus*, no. 3]. A timely invitation tailored to our centennial observance of the arrival in America of the first Missionaries of Our Lady of La Salette and aptly suited to the crossroads at which we now stand.

The Future of Our Present

The storehouse of our past—as the wrenching but trusting uprooting of 1892 testifies—is well stocked with adversity and resolve, impasse and imagination, dilemma and decision. In an economy of words, evocative and resonant with truth, the Holy Father articulates what we ourselves so strongly sense: our future holds equal measures of uncertainty and promise, of hesitation and hope.

Under the overcast of their own times, the men of La Salette a century ago looked to the brightness on the mountain. True to the cardinal rule of their life, which challenged them to see current happenings in its merciful light, they cherished the conviction that, come what may, the light shines forth more brightly because it breaks forth from the shadows.

At the beginning of this twenty-first century, *Centesimus Annus* enjoins upon every preacher of the Gospel the "current events rule" that has long stood as bedrock to the spirituality of the La Salette Missionary and as underpinning to his pastoral theology: "... part of the responsibility of pastors is to give careful consideration to current events in order to discern the new requirements of evangelization" [no. 3]. A pertinent reminder. It cannot fail to strike a responsive chord. Though history may not be as transparent as we should like, neither is it entirely opaque.

Neither a cinch nor the Sphinx's riddle, this ageless call to scrutinize contemporary events calls for demystification. If it is being proposed as indispensable to evangelization at this time, it cannot be a tantalizing but utterly impossible task. This simple, straightforward description offered by Richard John Neuhaus, author of *The Catholic Moment*, can perhaps help bring this imperative within our reach: "Each moment in time is equally close to God's purpose, and God's purpose is equally close to each moment. But we are to read the signs of the times to discern the obligations, limits and opportunities of our moment" [Neuhaus, 1989: 283].

We may be sure that evangelization in the late twentieth century will include a decidedly countercultural thrust. As long ago as 1975, Paul VI (1897-1978) identified evangelization with the transformation of culture: "The split between the Gospel and culture is without doubt the drama of our times ... What matters is to evangelize human culture and cultures ... in a vital way, in depth, and right to the very roots" [*Evangelii Nuntiandi*, no. 20].

What—we should truly wish to know—is furnishing the energies that motivate and move the people we address in our preaching, be it in spoken, written or witness form? What is providing people with their "criteria of judgment, determining values, points of interest, lines of thought, sources of inspiration, and role models" [Paul VI, *Evangelii Nuntiandi*, no. 19]?

"It is culture, not politics or economics or science or technology as such," Thomas E. Clarke astutely observes, "that provides the deepest energies shaping the course of history" [Clarke, 1984: 414]. An all-encompassing and pervading culture announces its secular gospel and renews its humanistic pledges of fulfillment and happiness each day. Who can honestly claim not to be a compliant accomplice?

As the traditional equation put it: Had Our Lady not appeared at La Salette, there would be no Missionaries of Our Lady of La Salette ... in the United States or anywhere else. Does this incontestable link with the Apparition relate—extrinsically and accidentally—merely to the historical origin of the Congregation or, does it relate—intrinsically and essentially—to its continued existence and ongoing revitalization? What implications could this equation have for us today? How might the Apparition, as a prophetic Marian intervention, assist us at this juncture in discerning "the new requirements of evangelization"?

If the message of genuine private revelations as compared with, and subordinated to, public revelation receives scant notice and is assigned minor significance, the question arises, as Karl Rahner noted, "whether anything God reveals can be 'unimportant'" [Rahner, 1963: 25] or, as Edward Schillebeeckx made the same point, "whether God could be telling us something we ought to know already" [Schillebeeckx, 1964: 192]. The conundrum has usually been handled by distinguishing between "new doctrines" and "new imperatives."

(from left) Karl Rahner, S.J., (1904-1984) and Edward Schillebeeckx, O.P. (1914-2009) were revered theologians and stretched and deepened our view of our Catholic faith; photo of Rahner: Jesromtel; photo of Schillebeeckx: Hans van Dijk / Anefo

Schillebeeckx further elaborated that in the instance of a private revelation "the dogmatic and moral content of the faith is confronted with present-day situations, in which it is 'necessary' for God, in love, to make [God's] concrete will, known in an exceptional and charismatic manner ... There is always in the concrete circumstances of our lives an ambiguous element which, especially in times of spiritual need, leaves us the choice between several courses of action" [Schillebeeckx, 1964: 193]. Those brave theologians who have ventured to treat of private revelations in a more than cursory fashion have situated them squarely in the arena of prophetic calls to action and emphasized that, "although all the subtle depths of psychology come into play in these revelations, God takes a direct hand in them" [Schillebeeckx, 1964: 192].

We should ask: Why is it that such "new imperatives," mediated by apparitions in response to critical moments in history, seldom get beyond devotional practices? Where did the Apparition cast its most probing light of prophecy—on the specific moral transgressions it enumerated; on the frequency and impunity with which they were being committed; on the incursions and inducements of a pervasively irreligious culture?

Our reading of the Good News that God takes sides for the poor and bids us redress the wrongs of exploitation and oppression should cause us to wonder whether the impoverished, long-suffering peasants of southeastern France were, in effect, being singled out at La Salette as the primary objects of heaven's ire. On the very bottom rung of their nation's halfhearted and inept economic restructuring, they were sinners sinned against, victims of government nonintervention and pawns of systemic injustice.

"In 1846, because of excessive summer heat and drought the cereal grain and fodder harvests were heavily damaged. Then in the autumn, heavy rains and flooding jeopardized the fortunes of farmers everywhere. The scarcity of wheat prompted commercial interests to remove most of it from the market. As the supply grew more critically short, higher prices would mean a handsome profit. The cost of bread skyrocketed; what meager resources they had, people spent on basic food items. Clothing manufacturers were forced to fire their workforce; the unemployment rate soared" [Tudesq, 1978: 392].

Critics have rightly made the point that, while the major Marian apparitions—inasmuch as the seers were chosen, for the most part, from the ranks of the illiterate and powerless—do mirror a Gospel priority, their traditional interpretation and the privatized devotion it has fostered, overlook the correlative call to transforming action [Pope, 1985: 195]: "If the apparitions had a prophetic mission, it only struck one social and political note. Although the visions appeared to the humble, they never carried a message of social transformation or suggested that the realm of Mary or the coming of Christ meant the overcoming of exploitation or oppression."

Can a general summons to penance and prayer, cast in almost abstract terms, hope to verify the essential definition of prophecy? Should not this call to conversion pinpoint the ills that are specific to a culture and time and prescribe concrete remedies? John Cogley wrote: "Nowhere else in the Church have the clergy been closer to their people than in the United States. Where they have failed, the failure perhaps was due in large part to the fact that they were too close and provided too clear a reflection of a people who were not only faithfully Catholic but uncritically American" [Cogley, 1973: 248]. Might there be some truth to his incisive comment?

How then should evangelizers go about decoding both the goodness of God's creation and the traces of radical evil in the complex strands of their own culture? Without such sensitivity, can evangelizers convincingly proclaim the transforming power of God's grace in a situation?

The search goes on for a creative, yet sound, theology of private revelations that will respect the radical distinction between normative public revelation and post-apostolic revelations, all the while validating the significance and necessity of the latter in and for the Church.

2012 General Chapter Mass with a worldwide group of La Salettes in Shrine Church, Attleboro, Massachusetts

As these pages have demonstrated, Our Lady's Missionaries consistently countered swelling tides of religious intolerance and secularizing influences with a renewed commitment to their preaching mission. In their struggle against identifiable contemporary evils, they seem never to have considered any drastic change in their basic approach or the adoption of any substantially new apostolate. At the height of the anticlerical onslaught, for example, they might well have directly addressed the shapers of public attitudes—the professors, legislators, journalists, whose effect on France's mores and psyche was wreaking havoc. They might have launched a massive letter-writing campaign, sought out university chaplaincies, rallied underpaid and disgruntled laborers, authored works critical of humanistic political trends or published articles warning that lost faith might never be recovered.

As was also pointed out here, they studiously refrained from sounding the apocalyptic trumpet, doom saying. or exploiting the dire predictions of the public message of La Salette. Not one single man crept over into the Melanist camp, attempting by means of lurid end-time images to stampede terrified souls back to the Church and into the arms of a loving God.

It does not entirely surprise us. then, that their firsthand experience of the concerns and problems peculiar to the American Church prompted no dramatic change in pastoral approach and led to relatively little ministerial innovation on the part of the early La Salette settlers in the United States. The special needs of the poor and unemployed, of immigrants and striking workers were met within the existing parish structure.

What specific contemporary ills the men focused on at the outset is difficult to determine at this remove. There was certainly no lack of lapsed Catholics around them, or of parishioners in Danielson, Fitchburg, Hartford and Phoenicia who missed Mass, worked on Sunday and took the name of the Lord in vain. But the sheer contrast between the fervent religious practice they encountered in this country and its sad decline in France undoubtedly gave them a brief and comforting reprieve.

Shortly after his assignment to Fitchburg as curate, Antoine Jolivet (1853-1928) shared his astonishment with subscribers back home [Missionnaires de La Salette, 1902:155]:

> "What a difference between this country and France! Over here, on a parish census of 3,700 Canadian Catholics fewer than ten of the men do not fulfill their Easter duty ... We have four Masses on Sunday and the church is filled for each of them. We preach at all the Masses, but the sermon is a bit longer at the High Mass. The church, which has a seating capacity of 900, is crowded for sung Vespers at 4:00 P.M. Very few children attend in order to make room for the grownups, among whom are a good number of men and young men."

Antoine Jolivet, M.S. (1853-1928)

Under normal circumstances, the Missionaries of Our Lady of La Salette might well have established a New World foundation eventually. The fact that persecution determined the moment of our implantation in America is a mysterious part of our history. A bold move by men of hope in painful and perilous times, it remains a compelling part of our heritage. Their faith conviction that the subtlest invasions of evil can effectively be met only by recommitment to the Gospel of merciful love is the most precious part of their legacy.

As we approach the next curve of our history's road, we read the signs of our own times to discern "the obligations, limits, and opportunities of our moment." Ministers of spiritual healing to a crippled freedom, building on what is authentically human and potentially Christian in our culture and on the pockets of the sane resistance our vowed lives offer to its excesses, may we provide—in the word we preach, in the ministry we do, and in the community we share—an alternative vision and concrete examples of a life that is modern, human, and Christian.

Their return again and again to the ministry of the word betrays neither a lack of creativity nor a loss of nerve on the part of those who came this way before us. It bespeaks a rare and remarkable fidelity to mission. Ever eager to annex mission fields at home and abroad, always willing to travel the parish revival circuit to enlist a wider audience for Christ's Good News and Mary's "great news," such men did credit to both acceptations of the title Missionary.

The charism of prophecy held them in its divine grip. In changing times and situations, it made ever incumbent upon them the sacred duty of alerting the People of God to the true nature of the danger their freedom courts when it chooses to exclude or forget God.

For Your Reflection

Scripture: Matthew 16:24-28 (The conditions of discipleship)

"Jesus said to his disciples, 'Whoever wishes to come after me must deny himself, take up his cross, and follow me. For whoever wishes to save his life will lose it, but whoever loses his life for my sake will find it. What profit would there be for one to gain the whole world and forfeit his life? Or what can one give in exchange for his life? For the Son of Man will come with his angels in his Father's glory, and then he will repay everyone according to his conduct. Amen, I say to you, there are some standing here who will not taste death until they see the Son of Man coming in his kingdom.'"

Questions for reflection:

- When did *you* grow up in your adult faith, accepting belief because you (not just your parents) wanted to believe in the Lord?

- What person or event in your life helped you to come to believe more strongly?

Prayer:

Mary, First Disciple of Jesus, your example of openness to God's call to be the Mother of God's Son is a signature moment in the history of humankind. Your continuing example of readiness to do

God's will is evident in the great events of our Christian history.

Help us, in your loving kindness, to reflect your faith and example in all that we say and do. May we absorb and live your message shared at La Salette and be dedicated ministers of reconciliation, and ambassadors for Christ, your Son.

We ask this through your loving intercession and through the grace of your Son who lives with the Father, and the Holy Spirit, one God, for ever and ever. Amen.

La Salette Invocation:

Our Lady of La Salette, Reconciler of Sinners, pray without ceasing for us who have recourse to you.

Sources

Acomb, Evelyn Martha, *The French Laic Laws (1879-1889). The First Anticlerical Campaign of the Third French Republic*. New York: Octagon Books. [1941] 1967.

Barrette, Eugene G. M.S., *A Search into the Origins and Evolution of the Charism of the Missionaries of Our Lady of La Salette.* Roma: Missionaries of Our Lady of La Salette, 1975.

Bassette, Louis, *Le Fait de La Salette*. Paris : Editions du Cerf. 1955.

Berthier, Jean, M.S., *L'Oeuvre des vocations á La Salette*. Grenoble : Baratier et Dardelet, 1884.

Bligny, Bernard, *Le Diocèse de Grenoble, Histoire des Dioceses de France #12*. Paris : Editions Beauchesne, 1979.

Clarke, Thomas E., S.J., "To Make Peace, Evangelize Culture", in *America* (vol. 150, no. 21), June 2, 1984.

Cogley, John, *Catholic America*. New York: The Dial Press, 1973.

Dansette, Adrien, *Histoire religieuse de la France contemporaine*.

Fr. Jean Berthier, M.S. (1840-1908), founder of the Missionaries of the Holy Family

    I. *De la Révolution a la Troisième République (1789-1879)*. Paris : Flammarion, 1948.

    II. *Sous la Troisième République (1879-1939)*. Paris : Flammarion, 1951.

Debidour, Antonin, *L'Eglise catholique et l'état sous la Troisième République (1870-1889)*. Paris : Alcan et Guillaumin, 1906-1909.

Doheny, William J., C.S.C. & Kelly, Joseph P. (eds.) *Papal Documents on Mary*. Milwaukee: Bruce Publishing, 1954.

Duggan, Thomas S., *The Catholic Church in Connecticut*. New York: The States History Company, 1930.

Galton, Arthur, *Church and State in France 1300-1907*. New York: Burt Franklin, [1907] 1972.

Giraud, Sylvain-Marie, M.S., *Le Livre des Exercices spirituels de Notre-Dame de La Salette*. Curtet, Jean, M.S. (ed.). Grenoble : Editions de la Revue des Alpes, [1863] 1946.

Gleason, Philip, *Keeping the Faith: American Catholicism Past and Present*. Notre Dame, IN: University of Notre Dame Press, [1987] 1989.

Greeley, Andrew M., *The Catholic Experience: An Interpretation of the History of American Catholicism*. Garden City, NY: Doubleday, 1967.

Guilday, Peter (ed.), *The National Pastorals of the American Hierarchy (1792-1919)*. Washington, DC: National Catholic Welfare Council, 1923.

Hennesey, James, S.J., *American Catholics: A History of the Roman Catholic Community in the United States*. New York: Oxford University Press, 1981.

Hostachy, Victor, M.S., *Histoire séculaire de La Salette: Un siècle d'or: 1846-1946*. Grenoble : Editions de la Revue "les Alpes," 1946.

Hostachy, Victor, M.S., *Les Missionnaires de La Salette*. Paris : Letouzey et Ané, 1930.

Ireland, John, *The Church and Modern Society: Lectures and Addresses*. Chicago, Ilinois: D. H. McBride, 1897.

Fr. Victor Hostachy, M.S. (1885-1967), a noted man of letters, has written many books about the history, missions and members of the La Salette Missionaries

Jaouen, Jean, M.S., *Les Missionnaires de La Salette*. Paris : Bernard Grasset, 1953.

Jaouen, Jean, M.S., *Sylvain-Marie Giraud (1830-*

1885): *Missionnaire de Notre-Dame de La Salette*. Roma: Conseil Général des Missionaires de Notre Dame de La Salette, 1985.

Jedin, Hubert (ed.), *History of the Church: Volume IX. The Church in the Industrial Age*. New York: Crossroad. 1981.

Kselman, Thomas A., *Miracles and Prophecies in Nineteenth Century France*. New Brunswick, NJ: Rutgers University Press, 1983.

Liptak, Dolores Ann, R.S.M., *Immigrants and Their Church*. New York: Macmillan Publishing Company, 1989.

Marty, Martin E., *Modern American Religion: Volume I. The Irony of It All 1893-1919*. Chicago, IL: University of Chicago Press. 1986

McManners, John, *Church and State in France, 1870-1914*. New York: Harper and Row, 1972.

McManners, John, *Lectures on European History 1789-1914. Men, Machines and Freedom*. Oxford: Basil Blackwell, 1966.

Missionnaires de La Salette, *Annales de Notre-Dame de La Salette. 1re série*. Grenoble : Maisonville et fils, 1865-1901.

Missionnaires de La Salette, *Bulletin des Missionnaires de La Salette. 1re année, n. 1-62e année, n. 603*. Tournai-Grenoble: 1902-1963.

Missionaries of La Salette. *Our Lady's Missionary*. Altamont, NY: 1939-1950.

Moynihan, James H., *The Life of Archbishop John Ireland*. New York: Harper & Brothers, 1953.

Neuhaus, Richard John, *The Catholic Moment: The Paradox of the Church in the Postmodern World*. San Francisco: Harper & Row, 1989.

Novel, Charles, M.S., *Du Corps des Missionnaires diocésains a l'actuelle Congrégation des Missionnaires de Notre-Dame de La Salette*. Rome: Missionnaires de La Salette, 1968.

O'Donnell, James H., *History of the Diocese of Hartford*. Boston, MA: D. H. Hurd Company, 1900.

Purtin, Malcolm O., *Waldeck-Rousseau, Combes and the Church: The Politics of Anticlericalism, 1899-1905*. Durham, NC: Duke University Press, 1969.

Perko, F. Michael, S.J., *Catholic & American: A Popular History*. Huntington, IN: Our Sunday Visitor, 1989.

Phillips, Charles Stanley, *The Church in France 1848-1907*. New York: Russell & Russell, [1936] 1967.

Pope, Barbara Corrado, "Immaculate and Powerful: The Marian Revival in the Nineteenth Century" in Atkinson, Clarissa W. et alii (eds.) *Immaculate & Powerful. The Female in Sacred Image and Social Reality*. Boston, MA: Beacon Press. 1985.

Rahner, Karl, S.J., *Visions and Prophecies: Quaestiones Disputatae #10*. New York: Herder and Herder, 1963.

Rumully, Robert, *Histoire des Franco-Américains*. Montreal : L'Union Saint-Jean-Baptiste d'Amérique.,1965.

Schillebeeckx, Edward F. O.P., *Mary, Mother of the Redemption*. New York: Sheed and Ward. [1954] 1964.

Shirer, William L., *The Collapse of the Third Republic: An Inquiry into the Fall of France in 1940*. New York: Simon and Schuster, 1969.

Fr. Jean Stern, M.S., is congratulated by Pope John Paul II for his publishing of "La Salette: Documents authentiques" (3 volumes)

Stern, Jean, M.S., *Constitutions et Règlements anciens des Missionnaires de Notre-Dame de La Salette*. Roma : Missionnaires de La Salette, 1968.

Tudesq, André-Jean, "La France romantique et bourgeoise 1815 1848" in Duby, Georges (gen. ed.) *Histoire de la France*. Paris : Librairie Larousse, 1978.

Will, Allen S., *The Life of Cardinal Gibbons. Volume I*. New York: Dutton, 1922.

Zeldin, Theodore, France 1848-1945. *Volume I: Ambition, Love and Politics*. Oxford: Clarendon Press, 1973.

Chronology (1846-2012)

1846

Saturday, September 19: the La Salette Apparition of the Virgin Mary to Maximin Giraud, age 11, and Mélanie Calvat, age 14, on the slope of Mount Planeau (approximately 6,000 feet high), while they were watching their herd of cows, not far from the hamlet of La Salette.

September 20: the first written account (the Pra narrative).

1847

Winter of 1846: the famine, begun in 1845, now rages through Europe. Controversies in the press. Major inquiries about the Apparition—the narratives of Logier, Bez, Long, and Lambert—are set forth.

September 19: at least 30,000 pilgrims go to the Mountain.

November-December: Bishop Philibert de Bruillard presides over the eight meetings of the canonical investigation commission on the truth of La Salette.

1848

Revolution in France: uprisings throughout Europe.

1849

Already 15,000 pilgrims have been inscribed into the Confraternity of Our Lady of La Salette, Reconciler.

1850

September 25: Maximin meets Jean-Baptiste-Marie Vianney, T.O.S.F. (1786 1859), the Curé of Ars.

1851

Controversy arises over the "secrets" given to each of the children by Our Lady.

September 19: Bishop de Bruillard publishes the Doctrinal Statement: the Apparition is authentic; public worship is authorized; a church will be built on the site of the Apparition.

1852

May 1, 1852: Bishop Philibert de Bruillard's publishes his second Pastoral letter, thus founding of the Missionaries of Our Lady of La Salette.

May 10: Arrival at La Salette of François-Michel Sibillat (1815 1870), former curate at La Tronche.

May 14: Arrival at La Salette of Pierre-François Denaz (1811 1857), former pastor of Saint-Jean d' Hérans.

May 20: Arrival at La Salette of Bernard Burnoud (d. 1865), former pastor of Corbelin.

May 25: Laying of the cornerstone of the shrine church at La Salette in France and foundation of the Diocesan La Salette Missionary Corps.

July: Corps. Philibert de Bruillard resigns as Bishop of Grenoble.

November 1: Arrival at La Salette of Pierre Archier (1815 1899).

December 9: Jacques-Marie-Achille Ginoulhiac (1806 1875) appointed Bishop of Grenoble.

December 21: Bishop de Bruillard announces that his resignation by-reason of advanced age has been accepted.

December 26: The appointment of Jacques-Marie-Achille Ginoulhiac (1806 1875) to succeed de Bruillard as Bishop of Grenoble is officially announced.

1853

April 23: Philibert de Bruillard enters his retirement at the convent of the Religious of the Sacred Heart in the Grenoble suburb of Montfleury.

Bishop Ginoulhiac publishes a Doctrinal Statement confirming Bishop de Bruillard's decisions and refuting objections by the opposition.

May 1: Ginoulhiac receives episcopal consecration at Montpellier.

May 7: Ginoulhiac is installed in Grenoble's Notre Dame Cathedral.

August 9: Ginoulhiac pays his first visit to the Mountain of La Salette.

1855

February 4: The Chapel attached to the La Salette Residence on Rue Voltaire in Grenoble is dedicated.

1856

May: Archier is appointed superior of the La Salette Missionary Corps.

1858

January 27: Community Retreat.

February 2: Albertin, Archier, Berlioz, Bossan, Buisson and Petit profess their first vows at the hands of Ginoulhiac in the chapel of the bishop's residence in Grenoble.

February 11: First of the apparitions at Lourdes.

July 16: Eighteenth and final apparition at Lourdes.

November 13: Sylvain-Marie Giraud (1830 1885), a priest of the Archdiocese of Aix-en-Provence, joins the La Salette Community on Rue Voltaire in Grenoble.

1860

February 2: Giraud takes his first vows.

December 15: Death of Philibert de Bruillard at age ninety-five.

1861

October 20: Giraud begins writing *The Book of the Spiritual Exercises of Our Lady of La Salette*.

1862

February: Giraud is appointed Master of Novices.

1865

February 2: Giraud is elected Superior General, all the while remaining Novice Master.

June 10: Giraud founds *Les Annales de Notre-Dame de La Salette*; the first issue reaches 1,000 subscribers.

1868

December 8: The First Vatican Council begins, summoned by Pope Pius IX (1792-1878).

1869

April 8: Bishop Bernard Bernard (1821-1895) is appointed Prefect Apostolic of Norway and Lapland with residence in Trondheim, Norway.

1870

March 2: Ginoulhiac is promoted to Archbishop of Lyons.

March 5: Pierre-Antoine-Justin Paulinier (1815-1881) succeeds him.

June 27: Ginoulhiac is installed as Archbishop in the Cathedral of St-Jean in Lyons.

September 2: Napoleon III (1808 1873) surrenders to the Prussians at Sedan. The Franco-Prussian War comes to an end. The Second Empire falls.

September 4: At the head of a revolutionary mob, Léon Gambetta (1838 1882) proclaims the Third Republic.

September 5: Paulinier is installed as Bishop of Grenoble.

October 20: First Vatican Council adjourned.

1871

January 17: Apparition at Pontmain.

February: A Monarchist majority is elected to the National Assembly.

March 18: The Civil War of the Paris Commune, an insurrection of radical Parisians against the pro-Monarchist National Assembly, begins.

May: In a week of bloody street fighting, 130,000 troops crush the Communard movement.

May 24: Georges Darboy (1813 1871), Archbishop of Paris, is arrested by the Commune and fatally shot while blessing his executioners.

September 17: The first La Salette Sisters Congregation is founded.

1872

July 27: The National Assembly passes a universal conscription law. Thanks to the Monarchist majority, seminarians are exempted from military service.

1875

March 1: Maximin Giraud, a witness to the La Salette Apparition, dies at Corps.

August 3: Amand-Joseph Fava (1826-1899), Bishop of Martinique, is appointed to the See of Grenoble, succeeding Paulinier, who was named Archbishop of Besançon.

November 18: Fava is installed as Bishop of Grenoble.

1876

Bishop Fava asks the Missionaries to write new Constitutions.

January 29: Giraud resigns the office of Superior General one year prior to the expiration of his fourth term.

January 29: General Chapter of the La Salette Missionaries.

February 10: Pierre Archier is elected Superior General.

February: General elections give the Republicans a solid majority in parliament.

February 14: First of the apparitions at Pellevoisin.

June 13: Fava makes his first pilgrimage to La Salette, climbing the mountain on foot from Corps.

August 4: Paul Bert (1833 1886) introduces a bill revising the Army Law of 1872 and striking all exemptions from military service.

August 5: Opening of the Apostolic School at La Salette - Corps.

October: General elections bring the Republicans a more resounding victory still.

December 8: Fifteenth and final apparition at Pellevoisin.

1877

Pope Pius IX invites Bishop Fava and Father Henri Berthier to seek Vatican approval of the Constitutions.

1878

February 20: Election to the papacy of Gioacchino Pecci (1810 1903), Leo XIII.

March 15: Jules Ferry (1832-1893). Minister of Education, files a comprehensive Education Reform Bill to which he attaches, as a rider, Article Seven: "None shall be permitted to direct a school of any kind, whether public or private, or engage in any teaching whatsoever who are members of an unauthorized religious community"; the intent of which he makes patently clear: "to close those institutions where students are taught to be counter revolutionaries and learn to hate and damn the ideas that are modern France's pride and *raison d'être.*"

August 4: Leo XIII issues the Encyclical, *Aeterni Patris*, calling for the renewal of Catholic philosophical thought on the basis of a revived Thomism.

October 8-9: Extraordinary General Chapter meets to discuss the advisability of taking on the Norway Mission and requesting pontifical status for the Institute.

November 21: At Castellammare di Stabia. Italy, Mélanie Calvat (1831 1904) writes a pamphlet entitled, *The Apparition of the Most Blessed Most Blessed Virgin on the Mountain of La Salette*, which includes a lengthy version of her "secret."

November 27: The formal petition for pontifical status is signed.

November 30: Bp. Fava countersigns the document; along with a copy of the *Constitutions*, it is forwarded to the Sacred Congregation of Bishops and Regulars in Rome.

1879

January: Republicans control the Presidency and the Chamber of Deputies.

January 15: General Chapter of La Salette Missionaries.

February 2: In Bp. Fava's presence, the following make their perpetual profession: Pierre Archier, Henri Berthier, Jean Berthier, Buisson, Auguste Chapuy and Joseph Perrin.

Archier is reelected Superior General.

March 6: The Congregation *de Propaganda Fide* entrusts the Norway Mission field to the La Salette Missionaries.

April 18: Laudatory decree issued by the Congregation of Bishops and Regulars confers pontifical status on the Institute *ad experimentum*.

April 25: Bp. Bernard Bernard receives the La Salette crucifix on the Holy Mountain and begins his "novitiate."

May 27: News of the conferral of pontifical status is greeted in all La Salette residences with the singing of the *Te Deum*.

July 9: The Chamber of Deputies votes to approve Article Seven.

August: The Apostolic School on Rue Chanrion in Grenoble opens.

August 20-21: The church at La Salette is consecrated and raised to the dignity of a Minor Basilica.

August 21: Solemn crowning of the statue of the Virgin Reconciler by Hippolyte Guibert (1803-1886), O.M.I., Archbishop of Paris and Papal Legate for the occasion.

November 15: Publication with the *imprimatur* of Salvatore Zola (1822-1898), Bishop of Lecce, Italy, of Mélanie Calvat's "secret."

1880

March 9: The Senate rejects Article Seven.

March 29: The Chamber of Deputies parries with legislation meant to enforce dead-letter laws against the religious communities.

June 18: A mission departure ceremony, honoring the first Norway contingent, is held on the Holy Mountain.

June 29: Expulsion of the Jesuits.

July 6: Bernard professes his first vows as a Missionary of Our Lady of La Salette.

August 2: General Council decision seeking a haven for the Scholastics outside of France.

August 30: Secret negotiations between Charles Lavigerie (1825 1892), Archbishop of Algiers and agent of Leo XIII, and French Prime Minister Charles de Freycinet (1828-1923) to obtain legal authorization in exchange for a sworn declaration of noninvolvement in politics by the religious are aborted when *La Guyenne*, a Monarchist journal of Bordeaux, maliciously publishes a report on the clandestine talks. A Royalist-Ultramontane bishop bears the alleged responsibility.

October: The State forcibly closes 261 religious houses and dispels 5,643 men and women religious.

November: Five men's congregations are granted legal authorization:

the La Salle Brothers, the Vincentians, the Sulpicians, the Paris Foreign Mission Society and the Spiritans.

December 9: An Accretion Tax Amendment to the 1881 State Budget is proposed: "All societies or civil associations must pay a tax on property left to them at the death of their members."

December 28: The Accretion Tax Amendment becomes law.

1881

May 28: In a 331 to 126 vote, the Chamber of Deputies enacts an Army Law abolishing all exemptions, but providing that public-school teachers and ordained clergy need serve in the military only one year.

October 15: Exodus of La Salette Scholastics to Loèche, Switzerland.

November: To the horror of the Right, Gambetta is appointed Prime Minister.

1882

January: In a final act as Premier, Gambetta lends his support to three years of compulsory military duly without exception whatsoever. Only twelve Deputies oppose the suppression of exemptions in the name of religion.

March: The Senate calls for the usual exceptions.

December: Death of Léon Gambetta.

1883

August: Ferry endorses the idea of Church-State appeasement on his own terms: "We have reduced the clergy and religious orders to submission, we are imposing obedience on the judges. We can now pursue a moderate policy."

October 23: René Waldeck-Rousseau (1846-1904) files a measure to enfranchise all common law associations, except those "between foreigners and French citizens" (that is, religious communities).

1884

December 21: The revived Accretion Tax Bill passes in the Chamber 393 to 89.

December 28: In a 155 to 90 vote, the Senate ratifies the Accretion Tax Law of 1884.

1885

January 8-February 2: General Chapter of La Salette Missionaries.

January 28: Debate on the Army Law resumes. The Chamber of Deputies focuses on a single controverted article: "the members of male congregations are to serve in the military."

February 25: Death by drowning of Henri Berthier.

March 30: The Army Bill carries 171 to 100 in the Chamber. The Premier, Jules Ferry, remains intent on securing a French protectorate over Indochina, where Catholic missionaries are useful allies. The Chamber bitterly attacks his policies and overthrows him when it learns of the evacuation of Longsan, Vietnam, then under French occupation. Charles de Freycinet, Prime Minister for the third time, succeeds Ferry and declares: "The religious question will lie dormant!"

August 22: Death of Sylvain-Marie Giraud.

1887

July 12: The Senate reestablishes the military service exemptions the Chamber of Deputies had eliminated.

Bernard resigns as Prefect Apostolic of Norway.

1888

April 6: By official decree, Fava entrusts the pastoral care of the Shrine at La Salette to Our Lady's Missionaries.

April 16: The Holy See confirms Fava's episcopal decree of April 6.

June 20: Leo XIII issues the Encyclical, *Libertas praestantissimum donum*, defining the nature and limits of human freedom, recognizing "modern political liberties," and admitting the principle of toleration.

1889

July 8: The approaching general elections and a shift in the mood of the French electorate pressures the Chamber to accept, 306 to 162, the Senate's version of the Army Bill.

July 15: The Army Law takes effect. "After one year of mandatory military service and training, the following are exempt from further military duty: in peacetime—young men who have obtained or are studying for the *licence* or doctorate, seminarians of the established churches, if they have become ministers before the age of twenty-six; in wartime—medical and ecclesiastical students are to serve as medics."

1890

May 14: Definitive approval of the Institute is conferred by decree of the Sacred Congregation of Bishops and Regulars.

1891

May 1-29: General Chapter of La Salette Missionaries. Auguste Chapuy (1826 1907) is elected Superior General.

May 15: Leo XIII publishes the Encyclical, *Rerum Novarum*.

1892

The Missionaries of La Salette withdraw from Norway.

June 8: Pierre Pajot (1860-1928) and Joseph Vignon (1861 1912) visit the Holy Mountain to place their journey and mission to the New World under the Weeping Mother's protection.

June 18: Pierre Pajot and Joseph Vignon sail from Liverpool aboard the *SS Labrador*.

July 2: The *SS Labrador* docks in Quebec, Canada.

July 9: Pajot and Vignon celebrate Mass on the feast of Our Lady of Prodigies in St. Joseph's Cathedral, Hartford, Connecticut: they have a conversation with the Cathedral Rector, William A. Harty (1845-1902). who arranges for them to meet with Lawrence S. McMahon (1835-1893. the local Ordinary.

August 12: Having heard the favorable vote of the episcopal consultors, McMahon welcomes the Missionaries of Our Lady of La Salette to settle in the Diocese of Hartford.

September 19: Mass is offered for the first time by the La Salette Community in the McFarland Residence, its new home.

1893

February-March: The La Salette Missionaries conduct their first parish missions in the United States: Jewett City, Stafford Springs, and Wauregan, Connecticut.

August 15: Etienne Cruveiller (1874 1945), Henri Galvin (1874-1962), and Constant Glatigny (1873 1905) make their first profession of vows.

August 21: Death of Lawrence S. McMahon.

1894

February 22: Michael Tierney (1839 1908), Pastor of St. Mary's in New Britain, Connecticut, is consecrated sixth Bishop of Hartford.

July 3-15: In France on business, Vignon reports personally to Chapuy and the General Council on the remarkable progress of the American Foundation.

October 7: In a well-attended ceremony, the cornerstone of the future La Salette College on New Park Avenue is blessed by Tierney.

October 11: The Missionaries of Our Lady of La Salette assume pastoral duties at St. Joseph's in Fitchburg, Massachusetts.

November 13: During a private audience, Leo XIII approves the belated vocations project presented by Jean Berthier (1840-1908).

1895

January 11: The General Council authorizes Berthier to pursue his project, the Institute of the Missionaries of the Holy Family.

March: The Premier, Alexandre Ribot (1842 1923), files a Subscription Tax Law calling for a percentage of 0.30 francs to be levied annually on the capital value of all property owned by the religious.

May 23: Our Lady's Missionaries take on the care of Our Lady of Sorrows Parish in Hartford, Connecticut.

September: Jean Berthier establishes the mother house of the Missionaries of the Holy Family in Grave, the Netherlands.

September 19: On the forty-ninth anniversary of the Apparition, La Salette College on New Park Avenue in Hartford is dedicated.

November 16-22: Conducted by General Councilor, Jean-Claude Villard (1845 1907), the first canonical visitation in the United States takes place.

December 3: The La Salette Missionaries assume the pastorate of St. James Parish in Danielson, Connecticut.

1896

A La Salette house of studies is founded in Rome.

The number of La Salette Sisters increases to 150.

1897

October 5: General Chapter of La Salette Missionaries.

November 15: Joseph Perrin (1836-1913) is elected Superior General. Pajot is appointed Vicar of the Superior General for the United States Region.

1898

May: Pajot returns to France to take up duties as Councilor and Secretary General, Vignon, is appointed Vicar of the Superior General for the United States Region.

July 19: Perrin's Circular Letter #3 advises that the Community has been fined for nonpayment of Subscription Law taxes.

September 16: La Salette College in Hartford, Connecticut, opens its doors to the first young American La Salette recruits.

1899

January 2: Death of Pierre Archier.

June 21: The Waldeck-Rousseau Government is formed.

October 17: Death of Bp. Amand-Joseph Fava.

November 19: Jules Morard (1867 1954) celebrates the first Sunday Mass in the new parish of Our Lady of La Salette in Alma, Saskatchewan (the Canadian Northwest).

1900

February 24: Paul-Emile Henry (1851 1911) is appointed Bishop of Grenoble.

April 13: Perrin's Circular Letter #8 exhorts the Congregation to fervent supplication and a renewed commitment to its charism in time of persecution.

May 18: Perrin arrives in Hartford to begin his first canonical visitation in the United States and Canada.

June 3: Blessing of the cornerstone of the new St. James' Church in Danielson.

1901

January 19: Perrin's Circular Letter #10 advises that the survival of the Institute and that of all religious congregations in France is at stake.

July 1: The National Assembly passes the Associations Law.

Late July: The General Council communicates the decision that the Congregation will not seek legal authorization.

September 15: A moving farewell ceremony is held in the Chapel of Our Lady of La Salette on Rue Chanrion in Grenoble.

September 20: The Ministry of Justice notifies public prosecutors throughout France that the period for filing requests for authorization would expire on October 3.

September 21: Exodus of Apostolics to Tournai, Belgium.

October: Casimir Gachet (1864 1941) and Jean Angelier (1870 1939) serve a twenty-five-day jail sentence for failing to leave l'Hermitage before the October 3 deadline.

The La Salette Generalate-in-Exile is established in Massongex, Switzerland.

1902

April 20: Our Lady's Missionaries take on the care of St. Francis de Sales Parish in Phoenicia, New York.

April 24: Paul Larocque, the Bishop of Sherbrooke, invites the La Salette Fathers to staff Sacred Heart Parish in Stanstead, Quebec.

August 19: The Federal Council in Bern moves to expel unwelcome religious congregations from Swiss soil.

The La Salette Generalate-in-Exile is provisionally transferred to Nocera, Italy.

September 16: Five newly-ordained Swiss La Salette Missionaries settle in Krakow to study Polish.

December 18: Clément Moussier (1860 1919) arrives in Santos, Brazil.

1903

April 29: The Tournai Apostolic School moves from the temporary shelter of the Sacred Heart Parish Youth Center to a residence of its own.

July 2-28: La Salette General Chapter at Villarfocchiardo, Italy.

July 20: Death of Leo XIII.

August 4: Election to the papacy of Giuseppe Sarto (1835 1914), St. Pius X.

August 19: Perrin's Circular Letter #11 offers a retrospective of recent convulsive events and their devastating effect on the Community in France.

1904

July 30: Diplomatic relations between France and the Vatican are severed.

December 19: Mélanie Calvat dies at Altamura, Italy (near Bari).

December 20: Joseph Fux (1872 1913) and Oswald Loretan (1876 1964) arrive in Hartford.

December 22: Fux and Loretan meet with Bishop Beaven of Springfield, Massachusetts.

December 29: Fux and Loretan take charge of St. Mary's Parish in Ware, Massachusetts.

1905

November 1: The American novitiate is transferred from Hartford, Connecticut, to Stanstead, Quebec, Canada.

December 9: The Law of Separation of Church and State passes.

December 11: The Law of Separation is promulgated. The Concordat of 1801 is abrogated.

1912

June 29: The Sacred Congregation of Religious issues a declaration to the effect that "the Fathers are to be recalled to La Salette, as is their right, as soon as circumstances allow."

1913

March 15: Death of Joseph Perrin.

August: Pierre Pajot is elected Superior General.

1914

July 28: World War I began; it concluded on November 11, 1918.

August: A circular issued by the Minister of the Interior suspends measures against the religious congregations of France.

From Belgium. Brazil, Canada, Italy, Madagascar and the United States, eighty-eight La Salette Brothers, Fathers and Scholastics, who had retained their French citizenship, enlisted in the Army of France. Sixty-three of them served in combat units. Many were wounded, and fifteen lost their lives in World War I.

1921

American La Salettes join their French brothers in Madagascar (Antsirabe).

May: The Holy See sends an Apostolic Nuncio to Paris; Paris sends an ambassador to the Vatican.

1926

Final approval of the Constitutions by Rome.

1927

American La Salettes found the mission of Morondava, Madagascar.

1934

The first division of the Institute into Provinces: France (Our Lady of La Salette), Poland (Our Lady, Queen of Poland), Hartford, CT (Our Lady of Seven Dolors), and Brazil (Immaculate Conception of Mary).

1935

La Salettes from Poland founded a mission in Argentina.

1937

La Salettes from the Hartford Province founded a mission in Arakan, Burma.

1938

La Salettes from Switzerland and Liechtenstein become a Province.

1939

World War II began in 1939 and concluded in 1945.

1940

July 10: Fall of the Third Republic.

1941

October 31: The Vichy Regime announces that all the expulsed religious may return to their homeland.

1942

July 9: Fiftieth anniversary celebration in Hartford of the arrival of the Missionaries of Our Lady of La Salette in North America.

In the presence of the Most Reverend Maurice F. McAuliffe (1875-1944), Bishop of Hartford, a Solemn Mass of Thanksgiving was celebrated in the Seminary Chapel by the Very Reverend Paul M. Regan (1897-1943), Superior of the Province of Our Lady of Seven Dolors.

1943

January 1: Our Lady's Missionaries return to the Holy Mountain.

In a 9:00 A.M. ceremony in the basilica, Etienne Cruveiller, Superior General, and Auguste Veillard (1895-1977), Provincial Superior of France, receive from the delegate of Alexandre Caillot (1861-1957), Bishop of Grenoble, the official document restoring the custody of the Shrine and mother house to the Congregation.

Speaking for many on this moving occasion, Louis Sorrel (1872 1949), Assistant General, said: "This joyful return to the cradle of their Institute calls the Missionaries of La Salette to be, more so than ever, the active and ardent messengers of Our Lady to her People, men brimming over with that spirit of prayer, penance and zeal the Holy Apparition so eloquently preached."

1945

The Province of the Immaculate Heart of Mary is established in Attleboro, Massachusetts, U.S.A.

1946

La Salettes from Switzerland found a mission in Angola.

Centennial celebration of the Apparition. Marian Congress in held in Grenoble and at La Salette.

1948

La Salettes of the Immaculate Heart of Mary Province (Attleboro) found a mission in the Philippines.

1961

The Province of Mary Queen is established in St. Louis, Missouri.

1962

October 11: The Second Vatican Council was opened by Pope John XXIII (1881 1963). It concluded during the Papacy of Pope Paul VI on December 8, 1965.

Various La Salette foundations in Italy form a new Province: Mary Mediatrix.

1967

A fourth United States Province, Mary, Queen of Peace, is established in Olivet, Illinois.

La Salettes from Hartford go to Argentina.

1968

Two new Provinces are established: Our Lady, Mother of Hope, in the Philippines and Mary, Mother of the Church, in Antsirabe, Madagascar.

1976

The mission in Burma is closed due to persecution and legally enforced attrition.

1985

June 6: Renewed and updated after the Second Vatican Council, the Constitutions are approved by Rome.

1988

In Madagascar the Province in Antsirabe and Region in Morondava merge to become one province.

La Salettes from India, educated in the Philippines, open a mission in their homeland (Kerala, India).

1990

La Salettes from Poland begin new works in Germany, Slovakia, Ukraine, and Belarus.

1991

La Salettes from Brazil, Argentina and Bolivia open a common novitiate in Cochabamba, Bolivia.

1995-1996

The 150th anniversary of the Apparition of Our Lady at La Salette. A year of celebration throughout the world.

2000

The four La Salette Provinces in North America (Milwaukee, Hartford, Attleboro and St. Louis) restructure into a new Province: Mary, Mother of the Americas.

2001

India is established as a Region.

2002

The 150th anniversary of Bishop Philibert de Bruillard's pastoral letter of 1852 that led to the founding of the Congregation of the

Missionaries of Our Lady of La Salette in his second Pastoral Letter, dated May 1, 1852.

2006

India becomes a Province.

2007

Angola founds a mission in Namibia.

2012

Angola is established as a Province.

Unification of the Swiss and Polish Provinces.

www.ingramcontent.com/pod-product-compliance
Lightning Source LLC
LaVergne TN
LVHW051836080426
835512LV00018B/2903